KU-595-420

London's Airports

Martin Bowman and Graham Simons

Pen & Sword
AVIATION

First published in Great Britain in 2011 by
Pen & Sword Aviation
An imprint of
Pen & Sword Books Ltd
47 Church Street
Barnsley
South Yorkshire
S70 2AS

Copyright © Martin Bowman and Graham Simons 2011

ISBN 978 1 84884 394 3

The right of Martin Bowman and Graham Simons to be identified as Authors
of this work has been asserted by them in accordance with the Copyright,
Designs and Patents Act 1988.

A CIP catalogue record for this book is
available from the British Library.

All rights reserved. No part of this book may be reproduced or transmitted in any
form or by any means, electronic or mechanical including photocopying,
recording or by any information storage and retrieval system, without permission
from the Publisher in writing.

Typeset in 10pt Palatino by Mac Style, Beverley, East Yorkshire
Printed and bound in India by Replika Press Pvt. Ltd.

Pen & Sword Books Ltd incorporates the imprints of Pen & Sword Aviation,
Pen & Sword Maritime, Pen & Sword Military, Wharncliffe Local History,
Pen & Sword Select, Pen & Sword Military Classics, Leo Cooper, Seaforth
Publishing and Frontline Publishing.

For a complete list of Pen & Sword titles please contact
PEN & SWORD BOOKS LIMITED
47 Church Street, Barnsley, South Yorkshire, S70 2AS, England
E-mail: enquiries@pen-and-sword.co.uk
Website: www.pen-and-sword.co.uk

Warrington Collegiate Learning
Resource Centre

A105633

London's Airports

Warrington

Contents

Introduction

Without airports no one would fly anywhere. Yet who wants to live next to one? For as long as people want to fly, there will be noise from airliners landing and taking off. And while millions of us enjoy flying every year, there is a noisy and sometimes distressing downside for the people who live or work near to airports and under flight paths. Many people get used to the noise from aircraft – just like people living near busy roads and railway lines get used to the noise from lorries and trains. But of course, there are those who are disturbed or annoyed by it. Yet thousands more take flying half-way across the world almost for granted. Air passengers have become almost blasé about the experience. But surely those queues at check-in were shorter last time you flew? Air passengers now have to be prepared for several bewildering hours queuing at check-in desks and passport controls, and endure the security checks before rushing along labyrinthine corridors to the 'gate' to board the aircraft and find the row where they are about to experience several interminable hours with fellow passengers. If they are lucky the in-flight meals and movies on the small screen in the seat in front help to pass the time.

Leaving Heathrow on a Boeing 747 to Australia is interminable, but it can seem even longer if having left Bangkok and cruising at 35,000 feet over the South Pacific the passenger beside you in the left-hand seat suddenly says, 'Do you know what plane this is?' When you tell him that it's a 747 he smiles, 'No, no, no, this is the *City of Edinburgh*. Of course, you always wanted to know this. But then he says knowingly, 'This is the same Jumbo that lost all four engines after flying through that volcanic cloud of ash off Indonesia a year ago.' The journey then resembles a scene from *Airplane*. You know the one – where the Japanese soldier with the bifocals commits hara-kiri rather than listen to the ex-pilot's war experiences in the Pacific.

And to think that a famous Brummie comedian once did a sketch about boredom on a flight to Oz when he started reading match-box tops to pass the time!

Everyone should have a hobby, but heading for Chicago, Detroit, Minneapolis/St Paul (the 'twin cities') and New York simply to stay at airport hotels and log airliner registration numbers?

Most of us want to check into and out of airports as soon as possible, and have little regard for the problems that go on behind the scenes. And who can blame us? BAA, the owners of Heathrow and now owned by the Spanish company Ferrovial, is increasingly caught in the middle of a conflict in which it has to cater to the British publics ever greater demand for trouble-free air travel, while at the same time paying heed to an increasingly powerful environmental lobby and ever stricter security regulations. Despite the complaints from passengers and airlines (including delays at security with overlong queues), overcrowding, poor signage and cleanliness, lost baggage, flight delays and the high cost of landing fees things are improving. Over recent years Heathrow has become a veritable 'city', with five terminals and with the demolishing of Terminal Two and the Queens Building for redevelopment, things can only get better. This colossal growth has all come under BAA. Over the next five years or so, most of the passengers using this airport will be coming through facilities that do not exist today. A quirk here is that BAA, is still widely, if erroneously, referred to as the 'British Airports Authority' by both the media and the public – even though the Authority was dissolved following the 1986 privatisation! The company is adamant that its name is strictly 'BAA Limited' and that the letters do not officially stand for anything.

But BAA's issues go well beyond aesthetics. In a recent survey conducted at Heathrow, during July and August 2009 (the latter a record month for passenger numbers), thanks to millions being invested in services and technologies to help reduce queues, 91% of the airport's passengers waited less than ten minutes to get through security in July, and that figure did not drop below 95% in August.

BAA has no responsibility for the usual snaking lines in front of the more popular check-in counters, or the embarrassingly long line of around two hundred disgruntled overseas passengers waiting in the Flight Connections Centre (FCC) for just four immigration officers to check their passports, while eight other counters are unmanned. BAA can only request – not demand – more immigration officers. Security queues are soon temporarily overwhelmed by the almost simultaneous arrival of two 747s. At Heathrow even with sixty-eight security lanes and 2,500 security officers employed, 250 more are needed, but that requires 10,000 applicants from whom to find 300 good recruits. Apart from new security officers to do more work and searches and increased security lanes, machines and detectors have been installed. New technology, such as the aTix machine from Smith Detection, the latest X-ray equipment able to detect explosives and liquids in baggage, has also been introduced.

Airports have to be policed. At Gatwick, for instance the District of Sussex Police are responsible for policing the whole airport, including aircraft and, in certain circumstances, aircraft in flight. The 150 officers attached to this district include armed and unarmed officers, and community support officers for minor offences. They also counter man-portable surface-to-air missiles by patrolling in and around the airport. A separate sub-unit has vehicle checks around the airport.

BAA is not responsible for restricting passengers to one piece of hand luggage containing no liquids, gels or sharp objects – another source of intense irritation. More than half of Heathrow's passengers, for example, still arrive with prohibited items, and nearly a quarter ignore the compliance officers who advise passengers what they can and cannot take on board before they reach the scanning machines. The airlines' responsibility is to load and unload the bags from their airliners, and 55% of bags miss their connecting flights because of delays getting them on or off aircraft. The airlines have an informal agreement with BAA to unload all bags within twenty-five minutes of landing, but the three British carriers – Virgin, BMi and BA – rarely achieve this more than 78% of the time in a peak summer month. And yet 76% of flights leave Heathrow within fifteen minutes of their scheduled departure times, and 23% within an hour.

CAA figures published in 2010 brought into sharp focus the very poor performance of UK civil aviation in 2009. With a throughput of 218 million, 2009 passenger numbers were down 17% to the levels of six years before. The CAA seemed to think that it could be a number of years before they reached their peak level again. At Heathrow, Gatwick, Stansted, Luton and London City the fall was 4.9% overall, with the largest declines in percentage terms at City (14.2%), Stansted (10.7%) and Luton (10.4%). Heathrow had the smallest decline among London airports, serving sixty-six million passengers in 2009 – one million fewer than in 2008. Gatwick handled thirty-two million passengers, down 5.3%.

Terminal 5 at Heathrow currently funnels sixty-seven million passengers a year through facilities designed for forty-five million. The £4.3 billion terminal, designed by Richard Rogers, is vast, bright and airy, with Britain's largest single-span roof, enough floor space for fifty football pitches, a six-platform railway station and 9,000 seats. Terminal 5 absorbs thirty million passengers a year, permitting the redevelopment of the rest of Heathrow. BAA could only begin its £6.2 billion investment programme when the Civil Aviation Authority, which reviewed BAA's tariffs for the next five years, allowed it to double landing-charges. Work started on Terminal 3's forecourt, and Terminal 4's refurbishment began when BA moved into Terminal 5. Phase One of a £1.5 billion terminal called Heathrow East is intended to replace Terminals 1 and 2 in time for the 2012 Olympic and Paralympic Games.

The XXX Olympiad will spotlight worldwide attention on the capital's main airports. Twelve and a half thousand athletes are expected to participate, watched by the holders of 9.2 million tickets – several thousand of whom will arrive in the capital by air. Many of these travellers will be first-time visitors with no experience or knowledge of London's airport infrastructure or facilities.

Olympic travellers, first-timers and seasoned air travellers alike will find much use for this book – for it sets out to provide concise, pertinent information on each of the five main London Airports, Gatwick, Heathrow, London City, Luton and Stansted, with a brief history of each.

From the Flight Deck

One of the leading operators of 747-series aircraft, British Airways has a scheduled route network covering around 170 destinations in almost eighty countries. On average, a BA flight departs from an airport somewhere in the world every ninety seconds, contributing to a total of over a quarter of a million flights in a full year, carrying over thirty million passengers and half a million tonnes of cargo.

Rain and strong winds hardly make a trip to the office any more enjoyable on a Monday morning, especially when heavy traffic and delays cause added frustration. However, knowing that British Airways 747-400 Speedbird 2019 will soon be your office at 30,000 feet and heading 4,941.55 statute miles westwards from Gatwick Airport, London, to DIA (Denver, Colorado) via snow-covered Iceland and Greenland does offer compensations!

Although the captain is in overall command of the flight, the operation of the 747-400 is a team effort. Apart from the flight crew, the sixteen cabin crew are on board to help ensure the safety of, and to look after, the 401 passengers seated in First (fourteen passengers), Club World (fifty-five) and World Traveller (332). (British Airways does not use the word 'class'.) The captain and first officers are required to complete a set number of take-offs and landings over given periods to maintain their currency. This is quite difficult to achieve on the long-haul direct flights, such as Gatwick to Denver, where flying times often reach nine and a half hours outbound and just over nine hours inbound. To qualify for a flight, it might be necessary for a pilot to operate the flight simulator if he or she has not carried out a landing within the last twenty-eight days. Automatic landings are only carried out when it is necessary, since only manual landings keep the crew member qualified.

On arrival at the aircraft, the various checks are performed. One of the pilots will walk around the outside of the 747 and ensure that everything is serviceable, making sure that no trucks have been moved into the side of the aircraft, that no pitot head covers have been left on, that the tyres are in good condition, that there are no hydraulic leaks, etc. The crew perform the cockpit pre-flight systems and equipment check, otherwise called a 'scan check'. Basically, this is done using the instrument panel itself as a check-list, and scanning around the panels in a pre-determined order, making sure that all the switches are in the right place, prior to departure. For the overall systems checks, the on-board computers, combined with the EFIS (electronic flight instrument system) displays, can be used for determining serviceability. Each check has to be satisfactory before the crew move on to the next item. Because just two flight crew operate the aircraft, the flight engineer duties have been built into the computers. The primary flight instruments are duplicated for both the captain and the first officer, so that either can fly the 747, and the communications and systems are located centrally for easy access by both crew.

They then request their slot times with Air Traffic Control (ATC). Slot times control the number of aircraft in particular airspace. Gatwick has just one runway, but it has as many movements as several large international airports with multiple runways. Once clearance is received to start up and push the aircraft back from the gate, the pilots then go into another check-list, to make sure that we have appropriate hydraulics systems pressurised (to provide braking and steering for the body gear). Then ground handling push the aircraft back and the flight deck crew start the engines, in the sequence 4-3-2-1, as No. 4 engine normally powers the hydraulics, which supply the main brakes. Autostart enables the pilot to start two engines at a time, and will take action if any start malfunctions occur. They then get clearance to taxi out. Turning away from the terminal, it is very important that only idle power is on, as too much thrust is powerful enough to blow a car over!

Gatwick is a very crowded place, and different holding points allow airliners to overtake each other to meet various take-off departure constraints. At its holding point, Speedbird 2019 is in queue for departure. When clearance is given, the aircraft is taxied onto the runway. Simultaneously, the pilots perform the last part of the before-take-off check-list, configuring the air-conditioning system and switching on the appropriate lights and warning the cabin crew by virtue of a chime that they are just about to take off.

Once cleared for take-off and accelerating down the runway, the non-handling pilot monitors the aircraft performance – whether you can stop, or whether you have to continue. This has been worked out during flight planning by calculating the speed to which the aircraft can accelerate (at its weight for the flight) and still be able to brake within the length of runway available. This speed is called 'V1' (V is for velocity). It is also the speed at which, if one engine fails, the airliner can still accelerate sufficiently to climb away safely from the runway on three engines. If the take-off has to be rejected prior to V1, the pilot closes the throttles, which routes full hydraulic pressure (3,000 psi) to the brake units. The brakes on a 747 are carbon-fibre, much the same as a Formula One racing car, except that there are sixteen individual brakes, one on each of the main wheels. The brakes have to absorb the energy for a rejected take-off of the aircraft at the maximum take-off weight of just under 400 tons and travelling at about 180 knots.

At V1 you are committed to take off. The pilot then removes his hands from the throttle levers and puts them on the control column. When they get to 'rotate' (VR), again using a calculated speed depending on the weight of the aircraft, the pilot initially pulls the column back smoothly to pitch the aircraft up to twelve and a half degrees – this over a period of about six seconds. If they rotate too quickly and pull the stick back sharply, there is a risk of striking the back of the aircraft on the ground. Also, the aircraft will not accelerate to the correct speed (V2 – engine out, safety speed plus 10 knots). VR and V2, calculated by the computer, are displayed on the flight management system (FMS). Conversely, if rotated too slowly, the aircraft will accelerate too quickly and will be at too high a speed, but also it will not climb quite quickly enough.

The lateral navigation path programmed into the flight management computer is then followed. Because of the noise abatement procedure, at 1,000 feet above the ground pilots reduce power to climb-power and at the same time accelerate the aircraft to its Flap Ten speed plus 10 knots. They then climb the aircraft using the computed speeds from the flight management computer (FMC), to the cruising level. All the meteorological data in the flight plan are then loaded, so that the FMC can compute a proper ETA at the appropriate altitudes that are going to be flown for the whole of the flight.

The weight of fuel on this trip is 120 tonnes, and a large percentage of this is carried in the wings. Once the centre-tank fuel is consumed, fuel is burned from the two main inboard tanks until they equal the amount of fuel in the outboard tanks. At take-off power the 747 burns fuel at a rate of up to thirty-two tons an

The First Officer takes a careful look at the front fan of an engine prior to passenger boarding. He is looking for any debris that may have been ingested or damage to the fan blades.

The First Officer checking all is well with the baggage and cargo hold prior to take-off.

Checking for signs of wear on the tyres or problems with the undercarriage.

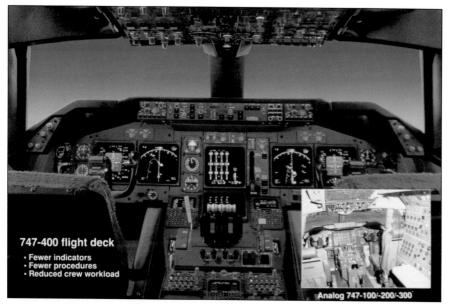

The digitalised instrumentation of a modern Boeing 747 400 Series compared with the older conventional layout.

The Captain and First Officer go through pre-flight cockpit checks.

The Captain takes the engine throttles in hand prior to take-off.

hour. At a cruising altitude of about 35,000 feet (using 20% or so of the available thrust), fuel consumption is reduced to ten to twelve tons per hour, or 3,000 gallons an hour. A 747 will typically burn seventy to eighty tons of its 143–60-ton fuel load (according to model) on the London–New York route (depending on direction and wind speed), while Qantas 747s burn up to 156 tons of fuel on flights of fourteen hours and forty minutes between Sydney and Los Angeles.

Speedbird 2019 flies on its routeing to the east of London, towards the Queen Elizabeth Bridge, then back west again, moving up, past Trent, Manchester, Nevis, Moray Firth and out towards the Western Isles and Stornaway, and then up over Iceland, out over Greenland, before coming in over Labrador, Hudson Bay and across the Canadian border into the United States and on to Denver. Greenland looks picturesque but distinctly uninviting as Speedbird 2019 passes majestically above the barren, rocky landscape at 34,000 feet. Outside air temperature at this height is minus 51°C. Even the fuel temperature is minus 64°F (-2°C). (Temperature falls with altitude at about 2°C every 1,000 feet, reaching about minus 65°F (-54°C) by 36,500 feet before rising slightly after this). With the 747s cruising speed of Mach 0.855, the temperature difference between outside air and the airframe (which is warmed by friction caused by the high-speed air flow) is 70°C.

As the senior first officer is going to do the landing, the captain takes control of the aircraft for the descent, handing over to the SFO again for the final landing, the SFO eventually disconnecting the autopilot and the auto-throttle for a manual, crosswind landing. This is because under certain circumstances the auto-throttle can destabilise the speed. Controlling the throttles manually allows a pilot to co-ordinate more effectively.

With a crosswind landing the pilot has to have the aircraft with drift laid off to maintain the extended centreline of the runway. Then as he approaches the flare manoeuvre, at about thirty feet above the ground, the aircraft is pitched up to reduce the rate of descent for a smooth touchdown. Then the nose is lowered towards the runway until the nosewheel touches down.

The senior first officer brings Speedbird 2019 in on finals to DIA at 130 knots in a gusting 25–30 knot crosswind that is causing a dust cloud on the prairie. On the horizon are the Rockies. At 14,000 feet a monosyllabic electronic voice booms out 'TRAFFIC! TRAFFIC!' (other aircraft are in the area). It is standard procedure in BA-400s that the handling pilot hands over the controls to the non-handling pilot for the descent. So in this case, as the SFO is doing the landing, the captain takes control of the aircraft for the descent, handing over to his SFO again for the final landing, on Runway Two Five at Denver. Although it does not look it from this height, the brand-new DIA, which replaced the old Stapleton Airport at a cost of a reputed $5.3 million, is the world's largest, at fifty-three square miles. Once we turn off, the after-landing check is executed and we taxi in towards the gate. At the appropriate time, a PA announcement tells the cabin crew to select the doors to manual so that it is safe for ground crew to open doors without the risk of the slides inflating and causing injury.

Speedbird 2019 lands at 14.28 local time, and is directed to its stand. The engines are shut down and the captain flicks the switches on the overhead panel. The 747 will be prepared for another crew and flown back to the UK on the next scheduled flight. After a lay-over in Denver, Speedbird 2019's captain and his crew will board Speedbird 2018 for an early-evening departure for London-Gatwick.

The first task for the senior first officer is to carry out the walk-around check. He checks the nosewheel gear for possible hydraulic leaks, and looks over the tyres for possible cuts and signs of wear and tear, and then looks inside the RB.211 fan engine to inspect the blades before checking the rear cargo hold. He also examines the control surfaces and checks that pitots and static vents are uncovered and that access panels are secured, as well as checking for signs of oil leaks, skin and surface damage caused by foreign object damage (FOD). The captain goes through the pre-flight check list with the first officer for the 16.00 departure to London-Gatwick. Because of the outside air pressure at Denver (which is 5,300 feet above sea level (asl) – not for nothing is Denver known as the 'Mile High City'), the AUTOSTART for two engines cannot be used. Instead, individual auto starts of each engine are carried out.

The captain taxies Speedbird 2018 out at Denver. Although the pan at DIA is huge (from the flight deck it looks certainly as wide as all eight lanes of the M25), he and the FO keep a sharp eye out for other aircraft. Having three pilots on the flight deck gives three pairs of eyes shortly before and during take-off. After rotate at 16.15 hours, while the captain and the FO pilot the aircraft, the SFO rechecks the fuel calculations. Speedbird 2018 heads eastwards via Chicago, Ottawa and Labrador, making excellent time crossing the North Atlantic, cruising

The view from the flight deck once the aircraft has been pushed back from the gate.

Looking down the runway about to take-off.   A final flight deck check

at 300 knots (525 knots ground speed) at around 32,800 feet, each of the three pilots averaging about two hours and twenty-five minutes in the 'hot seat'. At night, Speedbird 2018 overflies Ireland, crosses over Strumble, Wales, down to Portland, Chesil Beach at 27,000 feet, and the Isle of Wight and over the south coast of England at 12,300 feet, heading for Gatwick.

Track, heading, wind and distance on the last leg of the flight into Gatwick show up on the captain's navigation display (ND). Descent speed is 250 knots, and height is 11,400 feet. British Airways' Standard Operating Procedure (SOP) is to fly as clean as long as possible, for a continuous descent.

Outside the cabin window it is around minus 51 degrees Celsius.

A wonderful view from 34,000 feet.

The welcoming sight of Gatwick runway's landing lights.

The landing is on Runway 26L at Gatwick. The FO piloting Speedbird 2018 picks up the Glide Scope at 3,000 feet, ten miles out. At 1,000 feet the captain gets a feel of the controls and brings the aircraft in for landing. Gear is down at 7.45 a.m., and he puts the aircraft down with a gentle flare of two and a half degrees. Speedbird 2018 taxis to Remote Stand 171, and the engines are shut down. The two centrally located Engine Indication and Crew Alerting System Display (EICAS) display units show the fuel pressures, and that all four engines are shut down. The total fuel remaining is 10,100 kg. Chock to chock, it has taken nine hours and two minutes since leaving Denver, Colorado.

National Air Traffic Control Services (NATS)

Air traffic control for commercial flights started in 1920 when Croydon was first used as London's air terminal, but all the controller could do was give the pilot a red or green light for take-off and acknowledge position reports sent by radio. After the Second World War, ATC was the responsibility of the Ministry of Civil Aviation, and the network of air routes used today began to develop in the 1950s. National Air Traffic Control Services (NATCS) was established in December 1962, as a 'unified national organisation' covering civil ATC but liaising with the MoD (RAF) in areas where military traffic needed to cross civilian routes. National Air Traffic Control Services became National Air Traffic Services when it was made part of the Civil Aviation Authority (CAA) when that organisation was established in April 1972. Privatisation was first mooted in 1992, and although that debate came and went, it was recognised that as a service provider NATS should be operated at some distance from its regulator (the CAA), so NATS was reorganised into a Companies Act company in April 1996 and became a wholly owned subsidiary of the CAA. The Public-Private Partnership for NATS was proposed in June 1998 and enshrined in the Transport Act 2000.

NATS provides air traffic control services at fifteen of the UK's major airports (Aberdeen, Belfast International, Birmingham, Bristol, Cardiff, Edinburgh, Farnborough, Glasgow, Gatwick, Heathrow, Stansted, London City, Luton, Manchester and Southampton) and 'en route' air traffic services for aircraft flying through UK airspace. NATS competes for its business at the airports. Its *en route* business is regulated and operates under licence from the Civil Aviation Authority. The terms of the licence, available in full on the CAA website, require NATS to be capable of meeting on a continuous basis any reasonable level of overall demand. It is charged with permitting access to airspace on the part of all users, while making the most efficient overall use of airspace. In a year NATS can handle more than two million flights carrying over 220 million passengers. It is responsible for providing a nationwide network of communications, surveillance and meteorology services. Effectively this means the radar data for the controllers' screens, the radio frequencies they talk to pilots on and the ground communications between controllers. NATS also provides navigational services to airlines and the general aviation community.

The aviation industry downturn after 11 September 2001 led to a financial restructuring of NATS, involving £130 million of additional investment (£65 million each from the government and BAA plc), which reduced borrowings. BAA plc took a 4% shareholding, reducing the Airline Group's holding to 42%. Debt was further reduced by a £600 million bond issue, successfully completed in October 2003. In 2003 NATS launched its ten-year £1 billion investment programme with the announcement of a complete renewal of its radar network. Since then, it has been working with Nav Canada on a new system for oceanic control, entering service later in 2006, announced a study with the Irish into the development of Europe's first Functional Airspace Block, and launched a joint venture company with the Spanish to develop the next generation of air traffic management systems for Europe.

The guiding principle of air traffic control is that safety is paramount. Controllers must therefore keep the aircraft they handle safely separated using internationally agreed standards. This is achieved by allocating different heights to aircraft or by arranging certain minimum horizontal distances between them. These distances vary according to circumstances, but aircraft flying along the airways under radar surveillance, for example, are kept five nautical miles apart horizontally or at least 1,000 feet vertically. Within the airspace, a network of corridors or airways, usually ten miles wide, reach from a base of between 5,000 and 7,000 feet to a height of 24,000 feet. They mainly link busy areas of airspace known as terminal control areas, which are normally above major airports. At a lower level are the control zones that are established around each airport. The area above 24,500 feet is known as upper airspace.

All these areas are designated 'controlled airspace', and aircraft fly in them under the supervision of air traffic controllers. Pilots are required to file a flight plan for each journey, containing details such as destination, route, timing and height. Within controlled airspace, pilots must follow controllers' instructions; outside controlled airspace they take full responsibility for their own safety, although they can ask for assistance. In fact, military controllers, who work closely with their civilian colleagues to provide a fully integrated service to all users, offer an air traffic service to aircraft in uncontrolled airspace. Military personnel also provide services to aircraft crossing airways and for those flying above 24,500 feet. A priority task for them is aiding aircraft in distress. Aircraft in the initial or final stages of their journey are managed by controllers at the airport itself. When aircraft join the airways system, responsibility for handling them passes to colleagues working at the appropriate area control centre. A flight through their airspace could pass through several 'sectors' of airspace, each managed by a different team of controllers.

NATS provides *en route* air traffic management services to aircraft flying in United Kingdom and North Atlantic airspace, and handles civilian and military traffic from Swanwick, near Fareham in Hampshire, and Prestwick in Ayrshire. The London Terminal Control Centre moved from the area control operations room at West Drayton to Swanwick on 23 November 2007. One of the largest and most advanced air traffic control centres in the world, Swanwick entered operational service on 27 January 2002, when it began handling aircraft flying over England and Wales. At West Drayton, traffic in each sector was controlled by a small team of controllers, comprising a single tactical controller dedicated to each airspace sector, overseen by a chief sector controller position which acted in a co-ordination role. Swanwick, however, has two controllers per sector – the tactical controller and a dedicated planner controller – overseen by a local area supervisor and supported by an assistant. Through increased planning and co-ordination, planner controllers are able to resolve potential conflicts in advance, thereby reducing the workload of tactical controllers.

Swanwick controls 200,000 square miles of airspace above England and Wales, which is among the busiest and most complex in the world, with the exception of London and South-East area below 24,000 feet and the Manchester area below 21,000 feet. A total of 357 civil controllers (of whom ninety-three have also taken on extra training for supervisory duties), 170 civil assistants, thirty-five operational engineers, forty-seven specialist engineers and thirty-five military ATC staff (644 in total) have been trained to operate and maintain the system. This airspace is split into more than thirty flight levels, each separated by 1,000 feet in height. On a busy summer's day, the area control operation handles up to 6,000 flights. The operations room measures 2,000 square metres, half the size of a football pitch, larger than ten tennis courts, and three times the size of the room it replaces. The computer system has more than two million lines of software code – one of the most sophisticated IT projects in the country – representing over 3,300 functions, using twenty-three sub-systems connected by over thirty miles of cable (sufficient on its own to reach from London to Guildford), supplying information to over 200 workstations. Some 650,000 hours of testing have been conducted on the system.

Radar information is fed into the Swanwick system from nine sites in the UK. Five hundred telephone lines are used to support the operations. The centre expects to be continuously operational twenty-four hours per day, 365 days a year for the next thirty-plus years. The centre is the largest purpose-built air traffic centre in the world. It took five and a quarter million man-hours to construct, the largest construction project in Britain at the time. It has a floor area of 63,000 square metres, larger than most London department stores, and contains 400 miles of power and signal cable, enough to reach from London to Glasgow. It has forty-four miles of pipework (which would reach to Guildford from Brighton) and twenty-three miles of ducting (which would stretch across Yorkshire from Leeds to York). It has two five-megawatt standby generators in case of power failure – each sufficient to power two villages or a small town. It has a thousand smoke detectors and five hundred manual fire alarm call points. It is divided into compartments separated by walls giving two hours' fire resistance. It will maintain a constant temperature of 22ºC inside, through an outside temperature range from -10ºC to more than +30ºC.

The training programme took two man-years to prepare and involved over 21,000 individual assignments. Each controller spent 170 hours training on the Swanwick systems. It was one of the largest training programmes in the history of air traffic control.

Terminal control controllers in the terminal control room handle traffic below 24,500 feet flying to or from London's airports in what is known as the London Terminal Control Area. This area, which is one of the busiest in Europe, extends south and east towards the coast, west towards Bristol and north to near Birmingham. Controllers provide an approach service to aircraft inbound to Heathrow, Gatwick and Stansted, ensuring aircraft descend in a safe and orderly stream ready to land. At busy times aircraft are directed to holding stacks. Here they descend under the controller's guidance before being sequenced and released for their final approach. Aircraft flying from London's airports are handed over to terminal control shortly after take-off. The controllers then guide the aircraft into the airways, where they are passed on to staff in the area control operations room at Swanwick.

Terminal control is housed in a custom-built operations room at Swanwick. Controllers use full-colour monitors to give high picture quality. Computer-style on-screen menus, controlled by tracker ball, allow controllers to set up the required displays. Links to external data systems provide information on weather conditions, arrival orders of inbound flights and pending departures. Controllers handle flights to and from Heathrow, Gatwick, Stansted, Luton, London City, Northolt and Biggin Hill.

Military controllers provide services to civil and military aircraft operating outside controlled airspace. They work closely with civilian controllers to ensure safe co-ordination of traffic. Military services include aid to aircraft in distress, radar control to aircraft flying in uncontrolled airspace above 24,500 feet, and radar control of aircraft crossing national airways. To ensure the highest levels of safety, controllers need highly reliable equipment. LTCC engineers are responsible for maintaining integrated systems that support around 250 civilian and military ATC positions. Engineers operate comprehensive safety management procedures to safeguard these vital functions. System control ensures radar and radio coverage twenty-four hours a day, 365 days a year. LTCC engineers also run the National Airspace System – a computer system that holds a database of all scheduled flights and provides flight progress strips to the controllers. Engineers ensure that twenty-one transmitter and receiver sites provide radio coverage via more than 140 channels. LTCC receives radar information from twelve radar sites, as far apart as Heathrow airport and a site atop Great Dun Fell in the Pennines. Radar and radio information is continuously recorded for incident analysis.

The Airports

CHAPTER ONE

Gatwick

Gatwick was formally developed as a major airport in 1958 following an investment of £7.8 million, before which it was only used by a small number of commercial aircraft. It is the second-largest airport serving London and the South-East of England, and the second-busiest airport in the UK after Heathrow. The airport also has the distinction of being the busiest single-runway airport and ninth-busiest airport in the world in terms of passengers per year (handling nearly 34.2 million in 2008).

The name 'Gatwick' dates back to 1241, and it was the name of a manor on the site of today's airport until the nineteenth century. It is derived from the Anglo-Saxon words gāt, ('goat') and wīc ('dairy farm'), i.e. 'goat farm'. In 1891, a racecourse was created beside the London–Brighton railway, and a station included sidings for horse-boxes. The course held steeplechase and flat races. During the First World War the course hosted the Grand National. In the late 1920s, land adjacent to the racecourse at Hunts Green Farm along Tinsley Green Lane was used as an aerodrome. Following a change in land ownership, the aerodrome was licensed in August 1930. Surrey Aero Club was formed in 1930 and used the old Hunts Green farmhouse as a clubhouse. Redwing Aircraft Company bought the aerodrome in 1932 and operated a flying school. The aerodrome was also used for pilots flying in to races. In September 1933 A.M. (Morris) Jackaman, who owned several light aircraft, bought the aerodrome. He had bold ideas for its future, such as expanding it for use as a relief aerodrome for London (Croydon) Airport and for providing a regular service to Paris, using de Havilland DH.84 Dragon aircraft. Overcoming resistance from the Air Ministry, which was concerned about the cost of draining the land and diverting the River Mole, Jackaman oversaw Gatwick's transition to a public aerodrome, which was licensed for non-private flights in 1934.

Jackaman raised money by floating his company, Airports Ltd, on the stock exchange. Other revenue came from the Air Ministry, which paid for the right

This Comet 4B served British European Airways, Channel Airways and finally Dan Air before retiring in 1978. It was then used for training aircrew at Gatwick.

A typical day at Gatwick in the 1980s. A line-up of British Caledonian DC-10s, Delta Airlines and Pan-Am Tristars.

Dan-Air 727s and BAC 1-11s at Gatwick's South Terminal.

A Dan-Air A300 outside the airline's maintenance hangar at Gatwick.

A typical Gatwick apron scene during the 1980s with a Dan-Air BAe 146 and a British Caledonian BAC 1-11.

to use Gatwick as a diversionary destination at times when Croydon Aerodrome was inaccessible. In 1935 Hillman's Airways, which merged to form the company that became known as the original British Airways, made Gatwick its operational base, thus increasing its commercial viability and providing more finance. The aerodrome closed on 6 July 1935 to allow a terminal to be built. Jackaman and his contemporaries considered terminals at other aerodromes to be impractical and unsuitable for expansion, so a 'proper' one was planned for Gatwick, linked to a new railway station on the adjacent Brighton main line. The circular terminal building – reputedly in response to a throwaway comment by his father – was designed by architects Hoar, Marlow and Lovett in accordance with the design provided by Jackaman, who submitted a patent application for the concept on 8 October 1934. Advantages claimed for the design, which soon became known as the 'Beehive', included efficient use of space and greater safety of aircraft movements.

The terminal was built from steel-framed reinforced concrete, with brick layers inside and a Vierendeel girder with six supports running around the first-floor roof. As originally built, the interior consisted of concentric rings rings of rooms and offices with corridors between them to keep passenger arrivals and departures separate. Six telescopic covered corridors or 'piers' led from the main concourse, allowing six aircraft to be in use at one time. The 'Beehive' rises from one storey in the exterior ring to three in the centre. This central section originally contained a control tower, weather station and some passenger facilities; the main passenger circulating area surrounded it on the storey below. Baggage handling also took place on this floor. A restaurant and offices were on the ground floor in the outermost ring. The ground and first floors have windows of various sizes at regular intervals, while the former control tower was glazed all around.

The contracted opening date of October 1935 was not met, partly because of ongoing drainage problems, but a new railway station was provided on time in September of that year. The terminal was completed in early 1936, and it was in constant use until it became obsolete in the 1950s, as the airport expanded. A subway led from the new station to the terminal 130 yards (119 metres) away, ensuring that passengers arriving by train from London Victoria remained under cover on arrival until the time their aircraft reached its destination. Gatwick was thus the first airport to provide direct, under-cover access to the aircraft, and the first to be integrated with a railway station. Although Gatwick airport was officially reopened on 6 June 1936, flights to various destinations, including

Jackaman's proposed service to Paris, began in May with three flights each day, connecting with fast trains from Victoria Station. Combined rail and air tickets were offered for £4 5s., and there was a very short transfer time at the terminal (on some flights, as little as twenty minutes was needed).

Two fatal accidents in 1936 cast doubts on the safety of the airport. Moreover, it was prone to fog and waterlogging, and the new subway flooded after rain. As a consequence, and because of the need for longer landing-strips, the original British Airways moved to Croydon Airport in 1937. Gatwick returned to private flying and also attracted repair companies. It was requisitioned by the Royal Air Force in September 1939 for use as a flying-school and for aircraft maintenance. Although night-fighters, an Army co-operation squadron and later fighters were based at Gatwick, it was mainly a repair and maintenance facility.

After the Second World War, maintenance continued, and charter companies flying war-surplus aircraft started to use the airport. Most services were cargo flights, although the airport suffered bad drainage and was little used. In November 1948 the owners warned that the airport could be de-requisitioned by November 1949 and revert to private use. Stansted was favoured as London's second airport, and Gatwick's future was in doubt. Despite opposition from local authorities, in 1950 the Cabinet decided Gatwick was to be an alternative to Heathrow. The government said in July 1952 that the airport was to be developed, resulting in temporary closure between 1956 and 1958 for a £7.8 million renovation. The redevelopment was carried out by Alfred McAlpine. On 9 June 1958 Queen Elizabeth II flew into the new airport in a de Havilland Heron of the Queen's Flight to perform the opening. However, this event was preceded by Transair operating the first commercial air service from the new Gatwick on 30 May 1958, while a Jersey Airlines de Havilland Heron was the first scheduled aircraft to arrive at the newly reconstructed airport.

The main pier of what is now the South Terminal was built during the 1956–8 construction of Gatwick. In 1962, two additional piers were added. Gatwick was the world's first airport with a direct railway link and one of the first to use an enclosed pier-based terminal that allowed passengers to walk under cover to waiting areas close to the aircraft, with only a short walk outdoors. Fully extendible jet bridges were added when the piers were rebuilt and extended in the late 1970s and early 1980s. British European Airways (BEA) started flying from Gatwick. BEA Helicopters and BEA Airtours made the airport their base. British West Indies Airways (BWLA) and Sudan Airways were among Gatwick's first scheduled overseas airlines. The latter's Blue Nile service between Khartoum and London Gatwick was operated with British United Airways (BUA) Vickers Viscount aircraft. (At the time BUA was acting as Sudan Airways' technical advisers.)

From the late 1950s, a number of private British airlines were established at Gatwick. Transair was followed by Airwork, Hunting-Clan and Morton Air Services, and in July 1960 these merged to form British United Airways. Throughout the 1960s BUA was Britain's largest independent airline. During that decade it became Gatwick's largest resident airline. By the end of the decade it also became the airport's leading scheduled operator, with a 43,217-mile network of short-, medium- and long-haul routes across Europe, Africa and South America. These were served with contemporary BAC One-Eleven and Vickers VC-10 jet aircraft.

An Air Europa 767 departs. In the background is the jumble of buildings of the South Terminal.

In late November 1970 British United Airways was acquired by the Scottish charter airline Caledonian Airways. The new airline was known as Caledonian/ BUA before adopting the British Caledonian name in September 1971. BUA's takeover by Caledonian enabled the latter to transform itself into a scheduled airline. In addition to scheduled routes inherited from BUA, it launched scheduled services to Europe, North and West Africa, North America and the Middle and Far East during the 1970s and 1980s. This included the first scheduled service by a wholly private UK airline since the 1930s between London and Paris, in November 1971, as well as the first transatlantic scheduled services by a private UK airline to New York and Los Angeles, in April 1973. It also included the launch of the UK's first private scheduled air service to Hong Kong (via Dubai) in August 1980.

The driverless people mover that shuttled passengers between the North and South terminals.

In November 1972 Laker Airways became the first operator of wide-body aircraft at Gatwick, following the introduction of two McDonnell-Douglas DC-10-series tri-jets. Laker's DC-10 fleet expanded throughout the 1970s and early 1980s with longer-range series 30 aircraft which enabled the launch of Gatwick's first daily long-haul, no-frills flights to New York JFK on 26 September 1977. British Caledonian was also a Gatwick operator of the DC-10-30 wide-body, having introduced its first pair in March and May 1977 respectively. The airline eventually operated a small fleet of Boeing 747-200s as well, having acquired its first 747 in 1982.

Other independent airlines, including Dan-Air Services and Air Europe, played a role in the development of the airport and its scheduled route network during the 1970s, 1980s and early 1990s. Dan-Air – owned by parent company Davies and Newman – had been at the airport since it moved there from Blackbushe in 1961. Operating as a part scheduled service, part inclusive-tour airline, Dan-Air flew a wide variety of aircraft that fitted seamlessly into a huge range of charter requirements. Dan-Air eventually grew into the United Kingdom's largest independent airline until it was taken over by British Airways in 1993.

Air Europe was one of at least three airlines founded by Errol Cossey, who had previously worked for Dan-Air and later went on to create Air 2000 and Flying

The main span of the new jet bridge is lifted into position.

Colours. In 1989 a decision was taken that would place Gatwick at the centre of a European-wide operation. The parent company of Air Europe was International Leisure Group Aviation, which created 'Airlines of Europe (AOE) BV, a Dutch-registered company with shares of 130 million Dutch florins nominal value, all held by ILG. AOE was a true pan-European airline, with a federation of national airlines, each operating under the Air Europe format, and marketing Air Europe in the national market. Each national airline had strong local partners, a common aircraft fleet to produce a standard product, and the ability to operate mixed scheduled services and charter flights as appropriate. The fleet consisted of three Boeing 757-200Es, five 757-200s, sixteen 737-300s, two Shorts 330s and two 360s, six ATR-42s and eight Metro IIIs. In addition, another 22 757-200Es, thirteen 737-400s, 18 McDonnell Douglas MD11s, 22 Fokker 100s, two ATR 42s and two ATR 72s

The view from inside the jet bridge with a moving walkway on the right and a splendid view to the left.

were on order. The intention was that each national airline would be profitable on a stand-alone basis, but effective overall control – to the local extent possible – would rest with AOE BV. Airlines of Europe Management Services was formed to co-ordinate and supervise fleet planning, engineering, computer systems and finance.

Each of the national airlines had a strong local management, with the local chief executive responsible for maximising the profit potential and supporting AOE's activities in other markets. There was no limit set on the number of local airlines and partners, and ILG declared its aim to '... introduce the concept to every country in Europe, where profitable opportunities exist ...' This in turn was expected to increase profitability over and above the anticipated high levels of the individual airlines. In return, he would be able to draw upon the experience and attributes of AOE and the other local partners. Tour operators who participated as local partners were to have close informal contact and first call on capacity at local rates.

In the year ending April 1987, Gatwick overtook New York JFK as the world's second-busiest international airport, handling 15.86 million international passengers, 100,000 more than JFK. Passenger numbers had grown steadily

Boeing 747 *Boston Belle* of Virgin Atlantic on the ramp.

Low-cost carriers have revolutionised air travel this century, easyJet being a classic example.

since the late 1970s, as a result of several government initiatives, which included transferring all scheduled services between London and the Iberian Peninsula from Heathrow to Gatwick, and compelling all airlines that were planning to operate a new scheduled London service to use Gatwick instead of Heathrow. The 'London Air Traffic Distribution Rules' came into effect on 1 April 1978. The aim was to help put Gatwick Airport into profit by creating a fairer distribution of traffic between London's two main international gateway airports. The government also granted permission for a high-frequency helicopter shuttle service linking Heathrow and Gatwick, and this began on 9 June 1978.

As passenger numbers grew, a circular satellite pier was added to the terminal building in 1983. It was connected to the main terminal by the UK's first automated people-mover system (now replaced with a walkway and travelators). A new air traffic control tower opened in 1984. That same year the non-stop Gatwick Express rail service to London Victoria Station was launched. There was need for more capacity, and construction of a second (North) terminal with an area of 75,000 m² and costing £260 million had begun in 1983. The North Terminal was opened by Queen Elizabeth II on 18 March 1988, and was expanded in 1991 with a second aircraft pier. In 1994 the North Terminal international departure lounge opened. An extension to the North Terminal departure lounge was completed in 2001, and in 2005 a £110 million additional aircraft pier (Pier 6) opened, adding an extra eleven pier-served aircraft stands. Linked by the world's largest air passenger bridge to the main terminal building, it spans a taxiway, giving arriving and departing passengers views of the airport and taxiing aircraft. In 2000 a major extension to the South Terminal departure lounge was completed. In 2005 an extension and refurbishment to the baggage reclaim hall was also completed, doubling it in size. In May 2008 another extension was completed to the South Terminal departure lounge, and a second-floor security search area opened. The South Terminal, which now covers an area of 120,000 m^2, is used mainly by low-cost airlines. Many former users have moved to the newer North Terminal.

On 12 October 2009 Qatar Airways' daily Gatwick–Doha scheduled service became the first commercial flight powered by fuel made from natural gas. The Airbus A340-600HGW operating the six-hour flight ran on a 50-50 blend of synthetic gas-to-liquids (GTL) and conventional oil-based kerosene developed by Shell instead of traditional, purely oil-based aviation turbine fuel.

On 3 December 2009, ownership of Gatwick was transferred from BAA Ltd to Global Infrastructure Partners (GIP). Following the sale GIP announced its intention to proceed with a previously agreed £1 billion investment programme to upgrade and expand the existing airport infrastructure to firmly establish Gatwick as the London airport of choice for air travellers in the capital and South-East England. According to Virgin Atlantic communications director Paul Charles, the prospect of offering much better facilities to Gatwick's airlines and passengers as a result of the change in ownership presented a long-term opportunity to leapfrog Heathrow in terms of airport infrastructure and passenger amenities. A new twice-weekly Royal Jordanian service to Amman, with flights starting on 31 March 2010, appeared to be an early indicator that GIP's efforts to use its relationships to attract new airlines to the airport were succeeding. It was expected, therefore, that other airlines would also consider launching new routes from Gatwick.

British Airways and easyJet are Gatwick's dominant airline operators. The acquisition of GB Airways in March 2008 saw easyJet becoming Gatwick's biggest short-haul operator, accounting for 29% of short-haul passengers (ahead of

BA's 23%), and Gatwick's largest airline overall, with flights to sixty-two domestic and European destinations. By late 2008 Flybe had become Gatwick's third-largest slot-holder, accounting for 9% of the airport's slots, as well as its fastest-growing airline. Continental Airlines was the second transatlantic carrier – after American Airlines – to pull out of Gatwick altogether, following its decision to transfer its seasonal Cleveland service to Heathrow from 3 May 2009. The slots vacated by these moves, as well as by the collapse of Zoom, XL Airways UK and Sterling, were taken by easyJet, Flybe, Norwegian Air Shuttle and Ryanair. Gatwick is the airline's largest base, where its ten million passengers per annum account for almost 30% of the airport's yearly total. From a peak of 40% in 2001, BA's share of Gatwick slots have declined by 50% to 20% by summer 2009.

The runway at Gatwick is 3,316 metres long and 45 metres wide. Strictly speaking, Gatwick has two runways, but the northern one can only be used when the main runway is not in use, e.g. because of maintenance or an accident. The runways cannot be used at the same time because there is insufficient separation, and during normal operation the northern runway is used as a taxiway. It can

A queue of aircraft awaiting departure from Gatwick's main runway.

One of Ryanair's large fleet of Boeing 737s passes a Delta MD-11.

An overview of Gatwick's North Terminal with the control tower and main runway in the background.

Christmas in the North Terminal.

The South Terminal.

take fifteen minutes to change from one runway to the other. Night flights are subject to restrictions. Between 11 p.m. and 7 a.m. the noisiest aircraft may not operate. In addition, between 11.30 p.m. and 6 a.m. (the night quota period) there are limits. In 1979 an agreement was reached with West Sussex County Council not to build a second runway before 2019. In its original consultation document published on 23 July 2002, the government decided to expand Stansted and Heathrow, but not Gatwick. However, Medway Council and Kent and Essex County Councils sought a judicial review of this decision. The judge reviewing the lawfulness of the government's decision ruled that excluding Gatwick from the original consultation was irrational and/or unfair. Following the judge's ruling and the Secretary of State for Transport's decision not to appeal, BAA published new consultation documents. These included an option of a possible second runway at Gatwick to the south of the existing airport boundary, leaving the villages of Charlwood and Hookwood to the north of the airport intact. This led to protests about increased noise and pollution, demolition of houses and destruction of villages.

As of late 2008, both terminals were adapted to handle the Airbus A380 on a regular, commercial basis. Since 2008 BAA has spent about £100 million on the airport's development. The department lounge in the South Terminal was renovated, and security facilities and car parking facilities were improved as a part of the development. Expansion plans are receiving strong opposition from various groups and ministers. The risk of increased noise pollution, traffic pollution and water shortages are concerns. The airport saw passenger traffic of 25.3 million during the first nine months of 2009. In October BAA submitted planning applications for Gatwick to handle an extra six million passengers annually by 2018 and for an extension to the North Terminal to provide new check-in facilities and additional baggage reclaim hall capacity, along with a 900-space short-stay car park. Crawley Borough Council's decision to approve these plans was upheld in November 2009 by the government's refusal to hold a public inquiry, despite objections from local environmental protesters.

To reduce its debts BAA agreed to sell its stake in the airport, the news of which was announced by BAA on 21 October 2009. The deal was worth £1.5 billion, of which £55 million was conditional. Prior to the change of ownership, BAA planned an £874 million investment at Gatwick over five years, including increased capacity for both terminals, improvements to the transport interchange and a new baggage system for the South Terminal. On 2 December

Gatwick from the air. The main railway line to London or the south coast can be seen on the left.

2009, the House of Commons Transport Select Committee published a report entitled 'The future of Aviation'. With regard to Gatwick, it calls on the government to reconsider its decision to build a second runway at Stansted, in the light of growing evidence that the business case is unconvincing and that Gatwick is a better location. Several options to expand Gatwick have been considered. These include closing the South Terminal and building a new terminal between the two runways by 2020, and adding a second runway to the south of the existing runway. All this would allow Gatwick to handle more passengers than Heathrow does today. A less ambitious alternative centres on extending the North Terminal further south with another passenger bridge to an area currently occupied by aircraft stands without jet bridges (Pier 7). There are also plans to expand the capacity of the North Terminal and to extend Pier 6. A final master plan aimed at scaling growth in activity until 2015 has yet to be released after full review, but should be finished by 2011. The second purpose of this master plan is to draft preparations for the airport for the period 2016 and 2030.

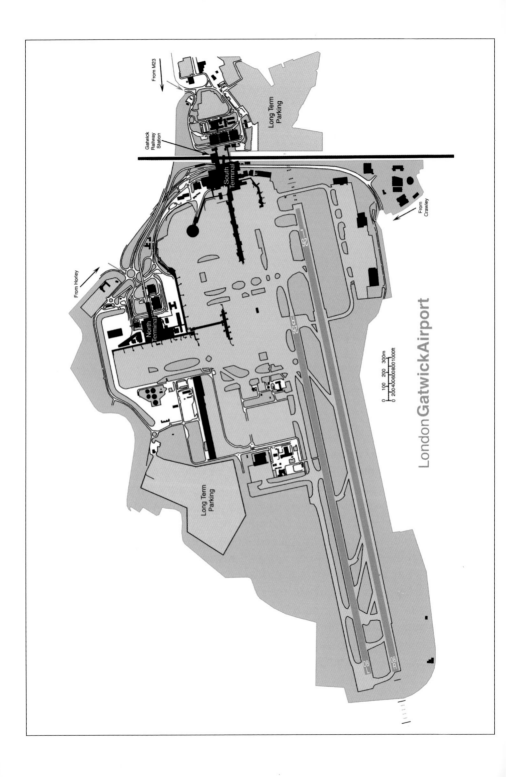

CHAPTER TWO

Heathrow

At 6.30 on Monday morning at Heathrow, in the Star Centre, a windowless central operations room lined with banks of screens showing Heathrow's many chokepoints, the first of three daily telephone conferences takes place in a day that will see about 210,000 passengers, 1,300 flights and 50,000 vehicles arrive or depart from the world's busiest international airport. On the walls in the room in the Star Centre are performance charts and a sign that declares, 'Delivering Operational Excellence'. It is a worthwhile aim, but probably unobtainable. At Heathrow more than forty airliners, each two and a half miles and ninety seconds apart, land every hour. A similar number take off on the parallel runway; Heathrow's two runways are used to 98.5% of their capacity.

Heathrow employs about 70,000 personnel, and when you take into account its larger community, the facility itself employs a total of 170,000 people, making it a truly vital part of London's economy. Six duty managers airside (DMA) look after the daily operations at Heathrow. This includes the runway, the taxiway and the stands. One of the DMAs specifically looks after the apron-area team and the manoeuvring team that facilitate runway inspections, bird-hazard management, marshalling, taxiway inspections, stand inspections and airside road inspections, and also operate procedures in case of emergencies and ensure that normal service is resumed as soon as possible. DMAs are on duty twenty-four hours a day, and they do twelve-hour shifts, days and nights. If they are on a day shift, the first thing they do is the handover from the night shift at 7 a.m. The departures start at 6 a.m., and arrivals will have been coming in since 4.30 a.m, so by the time they get to 7 a.m. everything is flowing as it should be.

All the maintenance on the runways, taxiways and stands is done at night, so if there are any issues or late hand-backs, then they pick those up and update the senior management team on the status of the airfield, whether there are any delays inbound and outbound, any flow restrictions and the weather for the day ahead. The foregoing is a snapshot of the operations of the start of the day, including any predictions or events that they know could affect the operation for the rest of the day. Then it's a case of checking to see if there are any other operations they might need to get involved with. DMAs have a diary where they log new areas of taxiways or stands that are being handed over. For example, with Terminal 5 there were always new stands opening on a regular basis. Before any area comes into live operation, the DMAs have to inspect it and make sure that it's compliant with all the rules and regulations, and that it's up to spec before they can sign it off to go live. They then check the diary to see if they have any events on for the day. Next, they check emails to make sure there is nothing else that needs to be seen to immediately. Other than that, they monitor what the inspection team is doing, so they are just ensuring that the routine inspections are done on time and as they should be. The rest of the day could involve attending meetings with various companies regarding operational issues.

On a night shift the DMA's role changes somewhat, to enable the airfield to become a large building-site to ensure Heathrow's vast development projects run successfully. For every area of work there is a permit for who is working there, their working hours and what they intend to do. DMAs work through those permits, sign them off and tick various boxes for the requirements that the contractors have to meet. They draw a map that shows the areas that are being closed off at night, and in the afternoon they take them all to the ATC tower to make sure they fit in with their evening and night-time operations, so that they can hand them over to the night-shift staff. The next task starts at about 9 o'clock. DMAs are responsible for enforcing the Department for Transport (DfT) noise rules, and so any aircraft that needs to manoeuvre in the night quota period, from 11 p.m. to 6 a.m., needs their approval to arrive or depart. DMAs manage the scheme under the instruction of the DfT. If an airline is running late because it has had to divert, or the weather is bad, DMAs check a database with every aircraft registration and its noise value. They have a set quota for the number of flights they can allow if they fit certain criteria. DMAs face a new challenge every day, and there is no leeway: the rules and regulations are very clear. There is also a lot of interaction with the airlines, and no two situations are the same. One airline can say that it has a problem with an engine, another with a passenger, and another has been diverted. DMAs have to think on their feet and cross-reference all the criteria.

The smooth running, therefore, of an airport the size and complexity of Heathrow is an unenviable task, and it is the domain of the operations director. The Star Centre receives reports from each terminal every fifteen minutes, and the operations director receives text messages on the length of Heathrow's queues every hour of every day, even on holiday. As a heavy flow of passengers begins and businessmen are flying off at the start of the week, he has to solve the trials and tribulations of the day. Engineers might report that two jetties for arriving airliners are out of action. The baggage manager might say that 300 bags that have missed connecting flights are lying in a reclaim hall. Several 747s full of passengers with onward flights will be arriving close together, so every security lane in the Flight Connections Centre must be open.

The flight director will receive no support from the press, which after one particularly bad summer of discontent led to *The Times* correspondent coining the phrase, 'Heathrow hassle', and another, 'a really expensive mall with planes'. Others weighed in with 'customer service reminiscent of the worst days of nationalised British Rail', and 'scenes reminiscent of Nairobi slums'. A BAA chief executive even described Heathrow as an airport 'bursting at the seams' and 'held together by sticking plaster' – before he resigned.

* * *

There has been an airfield at Heathrow since 1929, when Fairey Aviation bought 150 acres of almost level ground sixteen miles west of the capital near Harmondsworth, to provide itself with a flight test centre. However, one day in 1942 far-sighted government planners decided to investigate an area of London to be used as a civil airport. Surveys completed, approval was given for development at Heathrow, which meant that the owner was offered alternative accommodation at nearby Heston. In the event, Fairey did not finally move until 1944, the year when work actually began on Heathrow. The country was still at war and finance was tight, but the future needed planning for, so officially it was claimed that the airfield was needed for Transport Command in its support of the Japanese conflict; although in reality there were many suitable empty aerodromes in southern England now that the war had moved into Europe.

There is no doubt that there would have been much hostility directed against the government had it allocated millions of pounds to a civil airport scheme when at the same time it was trying to encourage the population with stirring words and deeds. The course of action taken was a practical and easy method of avoiding such unpleasantness, but leaving the way clear to provide the foundation for post-war air transport developments. By August 1945 Heathrow was beginning to take shape, with its main east–west runway and northern perimeter track already nearing completion, and so it was possible to announce the plans for Croydon's replacement without fear of censure. An Advisory Layout Panel was therefore created, its purpose being to produce recommendations for this airport of the future.

The RAF was preparing to take over its new station, and so on 13 October Transport Command Headquarters received a signal advising that an advance party should be established at Heathrow that would be a dependant of the main unit at Northolt. By 15 October accommodation had been secured for five officers and one hundred other ranks, with arrangements made for a twice-daily visit by the all-important NAAFI mobile van from West Drayton. The token force witnessed a visit of the British South American Airways' (BSAA) Lancastrian G-AGWG *Star Light* on 6 December, the aircraft remaining a few days before moving off to Northolt for maintenance. The RAF's short occupancy officially ended on 25 January 1946, when all personnel were withdrawn with the exception of seven drivers and two dog handlers, plus, presumably, their canine companions. From this point the Ministry of Civil Aviation (MCA) accepted the responsibility for all work. Strictly speaking the RAF had been lodging on civilian property, since it was on 1 January that the airfield was formally handed over to the MCA by the Air Ministry. That day was also marked by the first public appearance of BSAA when a Lancastrian departed on its initial proving flight to Buenos Aires. Nevertheless, despite the optimistically confident speeches by those entrusted to deliver such addresses, all was not well. Because of the wartime reluctance to disclose the real reason for acquiring Heathrow, the runway layout was obliged to conform to the traditional triangular pattern, all encircled by a perimeter track. This arrangement served well for the RAF, but it was completely unsuitable for the future high-density airliner movements envisaged even in 1946.

On the takeover day only the main runway, its parallel taxiway and the apron were ready for use. The two 6,000 ft strips running north-east/south-west and north-west/south-east still had some six months' work ahead of them, while two-thirds of the perimeter track had already been cancelled, despite it being at an advanced stage of construction. Other than at the ends, only two access points existed along the whole length of the operational 9,500 ft runway, resulting in some tedious taxiing to the inadequate expanse of concrete earmarked for aircraft loading. The close proximity of the Bath Road also meant that there was very limited space available upon which to expand the airport's buildings, leading to a very unsatisfactory ribbon development. Solid structures were a rare sight. With the exception of the control tower, which again bore an uncanny resemblance to many wartime specimens, hutted accommodation was provided as a temporary expedient.

Star Light returned from its sortie to South America on 15 January, with another Lancastrian leaving on the second proving flight six days later. The number of air services handled in the UK by this time was increasing to such an extent that Croydon was rapidly becoming overloaded, and since Heathrow was incapable of absorbing much traffic, the Air Ministry offered Northolt as a stop-gap measure. Long-haul services, including Pan American's new pressurised Constellation operating on the company's New York run, were currently terminating at Bournemouth-Hurn. Conditions there were nothing to get excited about, either, but at least Hurn did have a genuine military background to offer as an excuse.

On 25 March it was announced that Heathrow would be known officially as the London Airport. BSAA's regular schedule to Buenos Aires was by now leaving at 12.00 on Tuesdays and Fridays, although the passengers were usually government officials and other dignitaries. On 16 April this carrier lost its position as sole operator of the humble facilities when a forty-three-seat Constellation of Panair do Brazil landed to become the first foreign airline to patronise the new airport. Although only a proving flight, regular services were started shortly afterwards, the aircraft travelling via Paris, Lisbon, Dakar and Pernambuco. At last London Airport was coming alive, something that did not escape the notice of other carriers, particularly those with long-haul services. Originally it was intended that suitable accommodation would be made available before any influx of new operators was permitted, but under pressure the MCA allowed those using Hurn to transfer to Heathrow. On 27 May BOAC launched its first service when a Lancastrian set out for Australia. Another Lancastrian left on 31 May, when there was an inbound flight from Sydney. An Avro York destined for Cairo at midday was followed one hour later by an event of even greater significance. At 13.00 the first Pan American and American Overseas Airlines' Constellations arrived together from New York. Each aircraft carried thirty passengers, including the members of the 1946 United States' Wightman Cup team. It was an occasion that deserved some recognition, and as is so often the case, the British weather obliged with pouring rain! A gale-force wind blew it horizontally in sheets, drenching everything and everybody, including the luckless passengers as they dutifully posed for the historic portraits. Having endured this welcome, the next shock came when they were ushered into the collection of ex-military marquees erected in tidy lines for the use of airlines and their customers. Wooden walk-boards were needed to reach the entrances, while the rest of the area rapidly began to resemble a quagmire. Nevertheless, London Airport was formally declared open. By mid-June BOAC had transferred all its Empire schedules, which then totalled twenty-one per week. To these were added seven by Pan American, five operated by American Overseas, a couple of return flights by BSAA and a single visit by Panair do Brazil, which brought the total movements to over seventy per week.

Throughout this period the members of the Advisory Layout Panel had not been idle. They had the task of adapting a runway pattern known to be unsatisfactory into a design capable of handling the future traffic expansion. This had to be done at an operational airport in stages, to minimise interference with the airlines. It was considered essential that the three runways in an advanced state when the committee was formed in September 1945 should be completed with all speed. This part of the plan and provision of temporary buildings was thereafter known as Stage 1. The total area of land allocated for the expansion was about 4,450 acres (1,800 hectares), of which approximately 1,460 acres (590 hectares) lay north of the Bath Road. To bring the latter into the scheme meant that 924 houses in Harlington, Sipson and Harmondsworth would need to be demolished. Stage 2 should provide the maximum air traffic expansion to the south of the Bath Road, thereby postponing its diversion and the wholesale destruction to the north until the third stage. Once the general requirements had been agreed, the panel began to investigate runway alternatives in some detail. Two basic patterns were studied. The first was a tangential system around the central terminal, which offered the advantage of widely separated approaches, simplified taxiways and the ability to handle a high volume of traffic. It was a scheme already chosen for the new Idlewild Airport in New York, but it was considered that conditions in America differed greatly from those in the UK, and that it was not necessarily right for Heathrow.

Turning to the parallel pattern, this proved to be more suitable under the circumstances, particularly since the layout could be contained within the space allocated. By positioning the main runway on one side of the terminal, the building would effectively separate it from two others parallel but staggered, thereby allowing simultaneous take-offs and landings without the need for taxiing aircraft to cross the active strips. After assessing the space needed for passenger-handling buildings, customs facility, garages, car parks, communications centre and other essential services, all to be interconnected by roads, the panel members calculated that at least sixty acres would be needed initially. Another seventy acres had to be set aside at Stage 1 for airliner maintenance purposes, which at the second stage would increase to 170 acres, before finally spreading over 300 acres by the time that the airport was completed.

There was little in the final recommendations to generate renewed argument. Accepting the RAF triangular pattern as an established fact, the planners in effect positioned two separate layouts of similar configuration into the area, to bring the ultimate total of runways to nine, each direction possessing three in parallel, giving a result reminiscent of a Star of David. They were numbered 1 to 10 inclusive, the apparent arithmetical error accounted for by the absence of No. 3. This identity had been allotted to the north-west/south-east strip laid down as a part of the original pattern, which now had to be replaced to give sufficient room for the terminal area. Not all of the 2,000 ft length was wasted, since pieces were incorporated into aprons and taxiways. Dimensions proposed gave the main east–west runway a length of 11,570 feet, with its parallel partner 9,500 feet long, plus room for future extension. The others included in Stage 2 were designated as subsidiaries, varying in length between 9,200 and 5,800 feet. All were to be 400 feet wide, but it was proposed that for the time being taxiways could remain at 120 feet, providing they retained the capability for expansion to 170 feet when required. No reference was made of any access to the central area. No doubt the committee felt that there was no practical alternative to a tunnel. Only birds and aircraft could use other routes. Another snag with the island scheme concerned expansion. Unlike orthodox perimeter terminals, the amount of growth at some future date was limited.

By the autumn of 1946 a start had been made on the specification for the buildings. Having finished Stage 1 towards the end of the year, the contractors turned their attention to the provision of the parallel east–west runway south of the centre area. As planned, this activity did not interfere with the operational function of the airport, which by now was handling fifty movements per day, increasing steadily as new carriers arrived from Croydon. Following the example of other European operators, Air France arrived in mid-November. Iberia, Danish Airlines (DDL), Swedish Airlines (ABA) and Norwegian Airlines

(DNL) had already moved out, to be relocated at Northolt. Most of Heathrow's caravans and tents had disappeared, their place taken by temporary wood and brick buildings containing brightly decorated lounges and a buffet. Also, three temporary hangars were built for use until their permanent replacements were erected later. Each was capable of housing Stratocruisers, Constellations or DC-4s for routine maintenance.

By spring 1947 the Stage 2 runway pattern was taking shape. No. 4 was already well advanced and was intended as the replacement for the condemned existing north-west/south-east strip. Various taxi tracks to the permanent maintenance area had almost been completed at this time. Meanwhile, traffic to the continent increased. In June/July there were 957 movements for British-operated scheduled services, while foreign carriers accounted for 2,647 movements in the same period. It kept the pressure on for a speedy completion of the outstanding work, but the Ministry was forced by economic constraints to apply the brakes firmly at the end of the year. Up until December, 2,000 workers had been employed on construction, but following the call for drastic cuts in expenditure, this total had to be savagely pruned. Most of the surviving labour force was concentrated on building work or tasks essential to safety. During the year three runways were well advanced until work was suspended even before the general cutbacks. The north-side terminal would have to suffice for some years to come, yet in 1947 it handled 281,638 passengers, a figure growing all the time. Most of the effort now was applied to the east–west runway, as this was urgently needed to take over from the main runway when the latter was withdrawn from use tor tunnel work to proceed. A new customs area and a restaurant were constructed, while the cargo-handling accommodation also received attention, as this business was becoming quite substantial.

Long-term plans for the provision of hangars and a full maintenance base were announced in the summer. The scheme was expected to take up to ten years to complete, but during the first five the temporary structures already in use would continue in service. BOAC began using them early in 1948 for major maintenance checks on about thirty aircraft per week, in addition to other minor inspections. Initially three Yorks, three Lancastrians and up to seven DC-3s could be accommodated at any one time in the hangars. One was earmarked for Constellations, although the type could only enter sideways. Small trollies were attached to the wheels for this manoeuvre, a method subsequently used on many occasions elsewhere when the need arose. Pan American also required overhaul facilities in view of its considerable presence. An ingenious engine dock was therefore constructed, pending the erection of its own hangar on the south side. Consisting of two separate open-fronted sheds, it allowed the two engines on each wing to be maintained in comparative comfort. Equipped with light and heat, the dock was a great improvement for the engineers.

The first Pan American Stratocruiser to fly into Heathrow landed in April, and PAA began daily New York–London schedules on 16 August. Using Gander as a transit stop, journey time was fifteen and a half hours, but direct flights could be made with fewer than thirty-five passengers, which reduced journey time by forty-five minutes. At the end of the year BOAC introduced Stratocruisers on its American route, initially once a week. Frequency was increased until by the spring of 1950 the service became a daily event.

By spring 1949 the first two of four more hangars to house the new BOAC DC-4M fleet were under way. Though temporary, they were expected to give fifteen years' service. By this time 4,000 people, excluding 1,200 contractors' staff, were employed at Heathrow, and it was planned to recruit another 500. It was not an easy task to keep open an airport swamped with non-aviation workers. As

The Argonaut was one of BOAC's early post-war airliners. It was a Douglas DC-4, but powered by Rolls Royce Merlin engines instead of the American Pratt & Whitney radials.

A 1940s view of British Overseas Airways Corperation Boeing Stratocruisers at night at Heathrow.

many as 600 contractors' lorries were in action, all with drivers intent on proving that the nearest route between two points was indeed a straight line. Tracks had been allocated and marked out for the continuous traffic, but they were largely ignored by the earthmovers! To date the total cost of Heathrow was estimated at £8 million, leaving an optimistic £18 million for the future. No. 5 runway awaited only the diversion of two rivers at its western end before coming into service. No. 6 was 85% complete, with No. 7 about 70% laid. Clearance work in the centre area only began after the closure of No. 3 runway, itself dependent upon the replacement No. 6.

On 23 October 1950 excavations began on the all-important tunnel access to the central area. The 2,000 ft long subway was eighty-six feet wide, and contained two separate carriageways, each twenty-six feet in width, divided into two lanes. Two smaller tunnels were provided for cycle and pedestrian traffic. Owing to the nature of the subsoil at Heathrow, its construction was by the cut-and-cover method. In this way 600,000 cubic yards of earth had to be removed to allow the heavily reinforced framework to be built. Once in position, about ten feet of soil was replaced on the roof of the tunnels. One disadvantage was that the airport's busiest runway was out of action for many months, and there was a considerable increase in taxiing distance to reach the replacement No. 5. Coincidental with this activity, Holland & Hannen and Cubitts Ltd began construction of a maintenance base for BEA Viscount and Ambassador fleets from Northolt. Beam spans of 150 feet to support the main door openings were produced in position, unlike the main 110 ft roof beams, which were precast in sections at the factory. Assembled at the site, each weighed twenty tons when complete. BEA was able to make use of its new quarters by mid-1952.

Residents on the north side of the Bath Road had, since 1946, lived in expectation of a move to pastures new if and when additional runways were needed at Heathrow. At the end of 1951 the Minister of Transport said that it would be 1954 before there would be such a requirement, but the decision was taken to abandon all ideas for an extension to the north after investigations into the practical aspects of simultaneous landings and take-offs on parallel runways. Officially this change of policy was made independently of the selection of Gatwick as the second London Airport, although few people doubted that this did not have a direct bearing on the case. There was much jubilation among the residents of the 650 houses under threat, perhaps even sparing a little sympathy for the inhabitants of Crawley and Horley!

Passengers boarding a BOAC Comet 4 for the first transatlantic flight by a jet-powered airliner.

An aerial view of Heathrow in the 1970s.

In 1951 the de Havilland Comet 1 appeared at Heathrow when BOAC received the second prototype on 2 April so that development-flying and route proving on the sectors to India could take place. On 8 October, for the first time, a royal overseas tour started from Heathrow when BOAC Stratocruiser Canopus flew Princess Elizabeth and the Duke of Edinburgh to Montreal for the start of their Canadian trip. One of the most momentous events in the history of civil aviation occurred in 1952 with the departure on 2 May of a Comet 1 to Johannesburg in South Africa, at the start of the world's first jet transport scheduled service. Years ahead of the competition, the Comet gave Heathrow invaluable experience in handling airliners in the future.

In 1952 also, it was at last possible to observe the girder frames in the misty centre area. Most of the groundwork on aprons and subways had been completed, as had the runways and most of the taxiways. Both BOAC and BEA permanent quarters were also prominent on the south-east perimeter. Unfortunately the planners appeared to have overlooked the position of the north-side control tower, which was standing in line with Nos 4 and 7 runways, making take-offs towards the obstruction unnecessarily hazardous in the event of an engine failure. It was not until September 1953 that details of the new buildings were released. Three were to be erected in the diamond-shaped area available. In the middle was the control centre, the block from which the 127 ft high tower protruded, completion of which was expected during autumn 1954. On the south-east side and eastern apex came the first of the passenger terminals alongside the accommodation earmarked for aircraft and their support services. No problems were envisaged with capacity. All medium-haul traffic was calculated to fit comfortably for the foreseeable future. There was no intention of trying to squeeze in the long-haul carriers, who remained on the north side, and the next terminal expected to emerge was planned for domestic and European users only.

In January 1954 the latest new airliner visited Heathrow when a Britannia flew in from Filton. By mid-June the tower and its accompanying buildings were almost complete. More time would be needed on the fitting-out stage, but limited use was expected by the beginning of 1955, in time for the summer season. This was essential because on 30 October 1954 the last scheduled civil aircraft left Northolt before the airport reverted to military control once again. During eight years or so serving as a London airport, Northolt handled a considerable number of movements. As recently as March the figure had been 1,531 during the month, compared with 3,959 by its neighbour. Passengers totalled 26,476 against the 95,581 handled by Heathrow. The overcrowded north side absorbed the latest influx, until on 17 April 1955 the first commercial traffic was handled by the incomplete centre terminal. On that date the new complex took on the official title of London Airport Central, with the original site assuming the name of London Airport North.

Despite the provision of expanded parks, congestion was quickly experienced. The journey time from central London along woefully inadequate approach roads often exceeded by a handsome margin the time spent in the air on a city-to-city trip. It was not until 23 March 1965 that the M4 motorway spur into Heathrow opened. In those days aircraft taxied along the nominated lines before turning to come to a full stop. In this way there was no need when ready to depart for tractors and push-back procedures such as happens today. Passengers were shepherded along corridors, down a covered ramp before a short walk across the apron to the aircraft steps, although there were never sufficient numbers of these near gates, which resulted in the use of distant stands and the time-honoured bus ride.

On 16 December 1965 HM The Queen formally inaugurated Heathrow by unveiling a panel. Normal aircraft movements continued throughout the ceremonies, and passengers from some of the twenty-five airlines already established passed through the newly christened Europa Building, which had opened in 1955. With many large projects intentionally phased over a long period, few end up as originally planned, and Heathrow was no exception. To meet the revised requirements, a new committee was convened on 27 October 1955 by the Minister of Transport and Civil Aviation. Under the chairmanship of Sir Eric Millbourn CMG, the new group began to tackle the problems that had arisen since the 1946 panel's findings. No one could have forecast the growth in air transport that had occurred, or indeed the number of cars pouring into the central area. Already the busiest airport in Europe, Heathrow would grow in importance with ever-increasing numbers for terminating air traffic and transit flights. The committee had to create enough terminal space to handle about 5,700 passengers per hour, with additional bursts of peak traffic during the summer. Aprons had to be expanded to contain 105 aircraft parking stands. As many as possible had to be within walking distance along newly constructed piers. All of these facilities had to be flexible enough to be modified as experience with the operation of jet aircraft was gained. Freight also came under scrutiny, since a large area needed to be devoted exclusively to this growing business.

The Bristol Brittania was one of the world's quietest aircraft and was extremely popular with passengers. It became known as the 'Whispering Giant'.

Piston power still ruled in the early post-war years.

The Vickers Viscount was the world's first turbo prop airliner and Britain's best selling aircraft of all time.

Ample car parks for the 2,500 vehicles per hour using the tunnel were essential, so it was proposed that the existing south-east/north-west No. 4 runway east of the terminal should be withdrawn from use to make room for their construction. This runway was the shortest of those in service, and was not equipped for instrument landings. Slightly more controversial was the suggestion that the longer and well-used No. 6 runway could be sacrificed in the future. A change of policy resulted in a proposal to introduce the pier system at Heathrow. This was essential if there were to be any chance of the airport coping in the long term. New terminal buildings, too, were planned. One was to be predominantly for BEA's short-haul traffic, and was to be situated on the north-east face of the area, but had dropped back slightly in order of priority. Long-haul accommodation was considered to be the most urgent, with this building positioned on the south-west, where it would interfere least with other movements. All the points were based on an estimated handling capability of thirteen million passengers per year by 1970; a figure which was exceeded by two million. Aircraft size was responsible for the discrepancy, the estimated movements figure being more accurate at around 270,000 per year.

The new long-haul terminal was ready for limited use in 1961, the initial batch of travellers passing through on 13 November. Intercontinental passengers at last had satisfactory facilities for the first time in London since the end of the war. In the early stages it was only used for the departures of BOAC and its associate companies. Arrivals were handled in the existing short-haul terminal nearby, where special temporary arrangements had been made for this type of traffic. As it was likely to give foreign visitors their first impression of the UK, much care had been lavished on the design of the Oceanic Building. In layout it was uncomplicated, and employed a trickle-flow system for the passengers in both directions. Check-in desks were arranged on the ground floor for those outward bound, the second half of the same area allocated as a customs hall for arrivals. On the first floor, shops, bars and restaurants were provided in the large waiting-lounge. Access to most stands was by a coach from a fleet of new vehicles originally designed for the Ministry, but later taken over by BOAC. When fully opened in 1962, the remaining long-haul carriers thankfully transferred their affairs from the north side. Those included in the final move were Aerolineas Argentinas, Air India, El Al, Pakistan International, Pan American, Panair do Brazil and TWA, while Trans Canada joined them from the short-haul terminal. By the mid-1960s the running of such a large organisation as Heathrow was

Above: For many years transatlantic services were flown by a small monopoly of airlines, Pan Am being one of them.

Right: British Airways Boeing 747s. The original 'Jumbo Jet', it has given good service for many years and is still being manufactured.

The entrance to the road tunnel to the central terminals in the early 1960s. Apart from the two two-lane vehicle tunnels, smaller ones outside them allow cyclists and pedestrians to reach the central area.

becoming too complicated for the ministry concerned. A specialist enterprise was therefore established to take over the administration of the two London airports, plus Stansted and Prestwick. As the British Airports Authority (BAA), its task was to operate, plan and develop each site so that it became profitable.

Immediately it became responsible for Heathrow, the BAA found it had to resolve the capacity problem arising from the phenomenal growth in long-haul movements. Already the prospect of aircraft carrying 500 passengers was almost a reality. A new concept in design was needed, and by 1968 work had started on the latest development programme. This aimed to provide an additional thirty acres of stands for the anticipated Boeing 747 armada, taxiways and a 915 ft long pier leading to ten larger-than-normal holding-rooms. Construction was started on a building specifically intended to handle the arrivals traffic, allowing the bulging Oceanic terminal to concentrate purely on departures. Two years later, on 1 June 1970, the reconstructed facilities were opened in readiness for the new-generation jets. During the course of the work, the suggestion that No. 6 runway would need to be withdrawn was acted upon, the T-shaped pier crossing this strip as it stretched from the main building.

The 747 was already a familiar sight at Heathrow. Pan Am had introduced the type to the country on 12 January during a proving flight to five European airports with Clipper Constitution. On 21 January 1970 Pan Am began a scheduled 747 commercial service with non-stop flights between New York and London, when Clipper Victor completed the flight after Clipper Constitution had suffered engine overheating problems while taxiing at JFK. Pan Am did not enjoy exclusive use of the airport for very long, as TWA made a proving flight on 6 February, just before introducing its own schedules. Inevitably there were ground technical problems, which led to 747s occupying stands for longer than their allocated time slots, with the resultant congestion. BOAC therefore submitted a plan to the BAA for its own terminal away from the centre completely, probably on the south-west side. The idea was not adopted, but years later the scheme in effect became Terminal 4. Although the corporation was experiencing handling delays in the long-haul area, its own 747s were grounded pending the satisfactory conclusion of industrial troubles. Talks had been in progress on the subject of crew pay since July 1969, but no agreement had been reached by the time that the first of the 747 fleet was delivered in May 1970 for storage. In 1971 a compromise was finally reached, and everything was made ready for the first scheduled flight to leave for New York at 12.00 on 18 April, but because of a flight engineers' dispute BOAC was unable to dispatch its inaugural 747 revenue-earning service until 25 April. Operational teething troubles ironed out, the 747 settled down to become probably the most docile airliner using the airport. The long-haul area became a smoothly run operation, and confirmed the forecasts of the planners.

In 1966/7 recommendations had been made to modernise the Europa terminal. These included the all-important finger-and-gate system, with the addition of air jetties in due course. It greatly increased the number of near parking stands, at the same time giving far more passengers the benefits of boarding their aircraft directly from the building. On the north-east face, the third terminal was already taking shape. When completed in November 1968 it was proclaimed to be the largest specialised airport building in Europe. Initially transferred to it were the UK domestic and Channel Islands flights, but it became fully operational after the official opening by HM The Queen on 17 April 1969. Thereafter all BEA and Aer Lingus domestic and short/medium-haul services were handled by Terminal 1, the designation of this latest block. In the interest of standardisation the names Europa and Oceanic were also dropped, to give way to the straightforward identities of Terminals 2 and 3 respectively. Subsequently all three underwent redevelopment. For instance, Terminal 1 needed its domestic arrivals area to be enlarged with the advent of the Boeing 757. Special accommodation had to be provided for passengers using the British Airways shuttle services. Apart from the airside update, Terminal 2 had had much of its internal layout changed during its existence. A plan for a major external facelift was also announced during 1985. All of this produced an unofficial slogan that was often quoted: 'Alterations as usual during business hours'!

Providing efficient facilities for the masses moving in and out of Heathrow by air was all very well, but trying to squeeze everyone through the tunnel was not a method that would suffice indefinitely. From the earliest days, British Rail had contemplated laying a spur from its existing track at Feltham via a new bore to the centre area, but this line was already extremely busy and could hardly be expected to absorb additional frequent services. It became the responsibility of London Transport to provide a link with the underground network by extending its Piccadilly Line from the Hounslow West terminus, but the government of the day declined to offer any subsidy for this expensive project. In the Minister's opinion, the long-term success of the line would mean that it would become profitable and all outlay would be recouped. Many thought this unfair in view of Heathrow's national importance, but nothing could be extracted to help towards the £15 million cost, which had to be borne by ratepayers, since the Greater London Council was ultimately responsible for funding. Work started on the three-and-a-half-mile track in 1971, following the route of the main A30 road to a new station at Hatton Cross. This section was ready for opening in July 1975. By boring under the runways, the tunnel finally reached Heathrow Central in time for the first trains to officially operate in December 1977. All three terminals were joined by subways to the station, and so the long-awaited alternative access to the airport was serviceable.

Another of the topics included in the 1957 Millbourn Committee report was freight. The position of the future cargo terminal had not been finalised, but in the mid-1960s work started on this new important feature on the south-west side. Completed by the BAA in 1968, the building cost £8 million to construct. This figure included only the basic structure, since the various operators financed the fitting-out themselves to meet their individual requirements. The facility covered 160 acres and was directly linked to the centre passenger terminals by a road tunnel. Nearly 3,000 feet in length, its construction involved burrowing under both Nos 5 and 6 runways without interfering with the normal air traffic. It was

Magnificent Concorde, the world's only supersonic airliner, roars into the heavens. Now retired, they flew from Heathrow for many years.

British Airways' diminutive and elegant Concorde is dwarfed by her stable-mate 747.

just impossible to use the cut-and-cover method employed years earlier for the centre access roads. Designed to have a handling capability of 500 vehicles per hour in each direction, the 33 ft 9 in. diameter bore was never intended as a public thoroughfare, although London Transport buses used it on some routes. When opened, the cargo terminal was used by a large number of aircraft employed specifically for this purpose. After delivery by road to the appropriate company's depot, the outgoing goods were containerised and taken via the tunnel to the allotted stand for loading during turnarounds while passengers were boarding. Heathrow overtook Dover as the UK's major cargo gateway, with the 1984 visible trade figure reaching a value of £20,084.5 million. This amounted to 13.5% of that passing through all ports. It was ironic really that twenty-five miles or so to the east a similar thriving port once existed until the short-sightedness of some misguided groups forced the sea container traffic away from the London docks.

On 13 September 1970 a Concorde landed at Heathrow after diverting from Farnborough when weather prevented its return to its Fairford test base. Numerous complaints were received about the supersonic airliner's approach noise, but it was claimed that production aircraft would be quieter. A number of years passed, and supersonic travel became an everyday occurrence on 21 January 1976 when a British Airways Concorde set off for America, and at the same time Air France dispatched one of its Concordes from Paris. Several procedural changes had to be introduced to cater for Concorde. Dispatch reliability was affected by the supersonic airliner's parking position on the apron, and it was also necessary to afford it towing priority. Running up the Olympus engines was not possible without noise reducers, so a special 'hush-house', incorporating detuners, was provided to allow the operation to be carried out without annoyance to staff and residents, and two bays in the British Airways Technical Block 'B' hangar were modified to meet Concorde's routine maintenance requirements. While the aircraft continued to be a consistent user of the airport, movements were never excessive.

Statistics warned in 1973 that passenger figures were mounting each year, even allowing for the occasional hiccup due to the fuel crisis and recession. Overall the picture was one of growth, with saturation point becoming closer. There was little point in contemplating another terminal in the centre, since there was no space left. The only alternative was to break away from the island layout and to erect the premises on the perimeter. Available sites were not plentiful, but one existed on the south-east side of the airport which was conveniently close to the A30 trunk road. Planning work was commenced for the new building, once its position had been agreed, followed by a formal application for permission to proceed. A public enquiry, governmental pondering and detailed discussion with the local authorities accounted for many delays, but finally the go-ahead was given. Work commenced at once on the new apron, which was to cover 290,000 square metres, with the first excavations for the structural foundations beginning three months later, in September 1981. The BAA planners not only drew upon the years of experience gained from the existing terminals, but also investigated other airports' solutions to the ever-present battle with capacity.

One of the lessons learned was that it was essential to segregate incoming and outgoing passengers to ensure a much smoother flow and far less congestion. At Terminal 4, departing passengers enter the concourse at first-floor level to find sixty-four check-in desks stretched in a single line. After passport and security inspections, the traveller then has the freedom of a single 650-metre-long waiting-lounge. This airside concourse contains several refreshment areas, bars, shops and duty-free goods. Moving walkways connect with the various boarding points, seventeen of which, from a total of twenty-two, give direct access to 'wide-bodied' stands. Arrivals have a similarly streamlined operation on the ground floor. Undercover routes lead to train and bus terminals, taxi ranks and private car parks.

Heathrow's main road tunnel had met the expectations of the 1940s' planners by coping with 2,500 vehicles per hour reasonably well. Any hold-ups experienced were usually caused by car parks reaching capacity. At these times the east-bore

The Terminal end of Heathrow's original road tunnel.

The main railway that connects the airport to central London.

cycle road was often opened for taxis entering the area. Those leaving have to take the normal exit carriageway. In the event of emergencies either of the smaller subways can be used to keep a smooth flow of traffic. With the opening of Terminal 4 to air traffic, there was evidence of the much-needed relief for the central area. All British Airways' intercontinental services were being transferred from Terminal 3, together with the airline's Paris and Amsterdam schedules from No. 1. In conjunction with the Terminal 4 work, modifications also began to the rail link. A tunnel was driven from Hatton Cross to the new station before continuing to the centre to join up with the existing line. Trains completed the loop, travelling via Hatton Cross, Terminal 4, Heathrow Central, Hatton Cross to Hounslow West and London. A high-frequency service was maintained: at peak times only a four-minute wait was necessary before starting the forty-five-minute journey to the city centre.

Heathrow finally made a start on an overground rail link when it was agreed that a mass-transit system would further ease congestion at the airport. BAA signed a twenty-five-year agreement with Railtrack for the use of the twelve-mile mainline stretch from Paddington to Airport Junction near Hayes. To help create the Heathrow Express service, overhead 25 kV AC electrification was installed on the route, including Paddington platforms 3–12. BAA is responsible for the five-mile underground section from Airport Junction to Terminal 4, via the central area. At Paddington Station, the London terminus has two platforms dedicated to Heathrow Express and full airline passenger and luggage check-in facilities. Non-stop trains began running on 25 May 1998. Heathrow Express services are operated by a fleet of purpose-built trains, capable of travelling at 100 mph, leaving dedicated platforms at Paddington every fifteen minutes between 05.00 and midnight. Further investment in 2003 provided for a new stopping service in conjunction with First Great Western that takes an extra ten minutes between Paddington and Heathrow. Partly driven by the need for reliable transport for the large numbers of Heathrow workers living in west London (for whom special fares are available), the Connect service, unlike Heathrow Express, is part of National Rail. Heathrow Express gained access to Terminal 5 via a new spur connection. Mott McDonald constructed 800 metres of twin-bore tunnels, plus 1.3 kilometres of twin tunnel to reach the new station complex for T5 in the basement of Concourse A. Shafts and cross-tunnels provide for ventilation and emergency evacuation. The boring had to be carefully managed, as it passed underneath the existing London Underground Piccadilly Line in two places.

Terminal 4's ability to handle 2,000 passengers per hour in each direction allowed Heathrow's total capacity to increase to thirty-eight million passengers per year. Without doubt the 'star' of Heathrow for many years was the Concorde supersonic airliner, which operated from special stands at Terminal 4. Inevitably, the time came when the aircraft had to be retired, and on 22 October 2003 Heathrow ATC arranged for the inbound flight BA9021C, a special from Manchester, and BA002 from New York, to land simultaneously on the left and right runways respectively. The Queen consented to the illumination of Windsor Castle as Concorde's last west-bound commercial flight departed London and flew overhead on the evening of 23 October. This honour is normally reserved for major state events and visiting dignitaries. British Airways retired its aircraft the next day. G-BOAG left New York to a fanfare similar to that given for Air France's F-BTSD, while two more made round trips. G-BOAF flew over the Bay of Biscay carrying VIP guests, including former Concorde pilots, and G-BOAE flew to Edinburgh. All three aircraft then circled over London, having received special permission to fly at low altitude, before landing in sequence at Heathrow. They serenely taxied around the airport for forty-five minutes before finally disembarking the last supersonic fare-paying passengers.

The Air Traffic Control (ATC) tower, which at eighty-seven metres is twice as tall as Nelson's column, is a prominent feature at Heathrow. More than twice the height of the old tower, it offers better unobstructed 360° views of the airport for controllers. It was designed by the Richard Rogers Partnership and engineered by Arup. Starting in January 2005, prefabricated twelve-metre sections were then inserted under the cab, forming a steel mast and gradually building to the full height of eighty-seven metres. The tower is supported by a 4.6 m diameter steel mast and three pairs of cable stays anchored to the ground. The mast, which is encircled by a three-storey technical and administrative building, provides access to the visual control room via one internal and one external lift, plus an enclosed stairway. The tubular plated main core was shaped to accommodate lifts, stairs, services and electronics, and the three stays ensure the rigidity criteria for the radar systems. Because of its location in the centre of Heathrow, construction was engineered so as not to interfere with the day-to-day running of the airport. This constraint required the 900 ton, five-storey control room or cab section – which is twenty-seven metres high – to be moved almost two kilometres across the airfield to its final location. The cab section of the tower was prefabricated at a nearby site close to the airport's southern boundary before being moved to its final location in the central terminal area, near to Terminal 3. In October 2004 the operation by a specialised team to slowly move the cone-shaped top section along taxiways and across the southern runway and into place was carried out using three remote-controlled hydraulic 144-wheel flatbeds, which provided sufficient spread of the huge load to avoid damage to the airfield. The whole operation took just under two hours. The positions of the top of the tower and the lifting beams had to be accurately monitored as it was raised. An automated system using GPS, high-precision extensometers and laser technology generated the position data, which were collected and controlled by Leica Geosystems

GeoMos software. The structure was then slowly raised by the use of strand jacks until the first steel section of the tower could be inserted underneath it. The steel column, consisting of six sections, and the tower, were progressively raised one section at a time over several nights, while no aircraft were flying. The tower reached an important stage at the end of 2005 with a topping-out ceremony, with gold bolts being tightened ceremoniously at the base of the tower to mark the completion of the main structure. The fifty-five Heathrow air traffic controllers moved into the £50 million tower in the last quarter of 2006/7.

In a speech to the Town and Country Planning Conference at Manchester Airport in November 2006, Lord Soley of Hammersmith, one of the most fervent campaigners for the future of Heathrow, announced, 'I first became concerned about the future of Heathrow in 1999, when I warned that Heathrow could collapse like the London docks unless we addressed the issue of expansion; but expansion in the context of modernisation and greater sustainability ... Yet people still say the future of Heathrow is safe because of the high volume of passengers. Heathrow Airport will have ample terminal capacity but too little runway capacity to keep up with demand.' Soley used the example of the London docks in the 1960s, which were beating all previous records in terms of imported tonnage, but by 1980 had closed because of constraints with technical and economic change. 'Now that Munich has overtaken Heathrow in the number of destinations served, [which has pushed Heathrow back] into fourth place in Europe, people are beginning to pay attention. Soon Milan, Rome and Madrid will overtake us, pushing Heathrow into eighth position in Europe.'

Some of the growth demanded at Heathrow was taken by Stansted, but the BAA and the government outlined plans for a fifth terminal at Heathrow, which after much discussion, planning wrangles and delays finally came into operation in 2008, nineteen years after its conception. Situated between the northern and southern runways at the western end of Heathrow, Terminal 5 was opened by Queen Elizabeth II on 14 March. It opened for passenger use on 27 March, but the first two weeks of operation were disrupted by problems with IT systems and insufficient testing and staff training, which caused over 500 flights to be cancelled. Terminal 5 is used exclusively by British Airways as its global hub. Built at a cost of £4.3 billion and designed by the Richard Rogers Partnership, it consists of a four-storey main terminal building (Concourse A) and two satellite buildings linked to the main terminal by an underground people-mover transit system. The first satellite (Concourse B) includes dedicated aircraft stands for

Two views of the interior of Heathrow's new Terminal Five, showing the main concourse (above) and check-in area (below).

British Airways' new terminal – now running smoothly after initial hitches.

the Airbus A380; Concourse C opened in 2010. In total, Terminal 5 has an area of 353,020 square metres, sixty aircraft stands and capacity for thirty million passengers annually. There are more than a hundred shops and restaurants. A further building, similar in size to Concourse C, may yet be constructed to the east of the existing site, providing another sixteen stands. This is likely to become a priority if British Airways' merger with Iberia proceeds, since both airlines will want to be accommodated at Heathrow under one roof in order to maximise the cost savings that the merger envisages. The transport network around the airport has been extended to cope with the increase in passenger numbers. A dedicated motorway spur has been built from the M25 between Junctions 14 and 15 to the terminal, which includes a 3,800-space multi-storey car park. A more distant long-stay car park for business passengers will be linked to the terminal by a personal rapid transit system, which is expected to become operational during 2010. New branches of both the Heathrow Express and the Underground's Piccadilly Line serve a new shared Heathrow Terminal 5 station.

On 23 November 2009, Terminal 2, Heathrow's oldest terminal, which opened as the Europa Building in 1955, closed, the last flight to depart being an Air France flight to Paris. Despite the best efforts of maintenance staff and various renovations and upgrades, the building was becoming increasingly decrepit and unserviceable. Originally designed to handle around 1.2 million passengers annually, in its final years of operation it often catered for around eight million passengers. After demolition, the building of a vast new Terminal 2 that would incorporate the site of the old Queen's Building, which was also demolished, was begun. This new home for Star Alliance carriers is expected to open in 2014. A second phase, replacing Terminal 1, will open in 2019. The construction of the new terminal envisages a complete realignment of piers more logically, and the building of new ones on the now defunct crosswind runway, in a site taking up roughly the same amount of space as Terminal 5. Formerly Heathrow East, the core terminal building will be known as Terminal 2A, and there will be two satellite buildings named Terminal 2B and Terminal 2C. Terminal 2B will provide Heathrow with sixteen additional stands, and it will be connected via an underground link to the main terminal building. Terminal 2C will be built as part of the second phase of the development. The entire project will have a capacity of thirty million passengers a year, and will cost £1–1.5 billion.

The major businesses operating at Heathrow, in particular British Airways and the airport operator BAA, long advocated construction of a new third runway at Heathrow, together with a sixth terminal, which would increase the capacity of Heathrow by 50%. Heathrow currently has only two parallel runways, operating at around 98% capacity. Its European rivals, such as Munich, Schiphol, Charles de Gaulle and Frankfurt, have runways operating at an average of only 75% capacity. If Heathrow was to maintain its position in Europe's airport hierarchy, it needed to have a third runway in the long term, and to operate in mixed mode (where the two runways are used for both take-offs and landings) on its runways in the short term, which would increase capacity from 473,000 operations a year to 573,000. Heathrow's two runways currently operate on segregated mode. One of the objections to T5 had been that it would attract fresh traffic that would demand an additional runway. Theoretically a 2,000-metre third runway operating in mixed mode would allow the airport to handle up to 720,000 movements a year. BAA estimated that the economic benefits for the wider economy of a third runway was £7 billion a year, or £30 billion by 2030. The government calculated that the proposal would generate over £4.8 billion in direct net economic benefits. On 16 December 2003 the Transport Secretary, Alistair Darling, released a White

Paper entitled, 'The Future of Air Transport in the UK', which reinforced the view that Heathrow was much more than 'just an airport' for London. While Heathrow delivered significant direct/indirect benefits to local and national economies, the government recognised that 'these strong economic arguments must be weighed against serious environmental disadvantages', and the White Paper set out stringent air quality targets, which would have to be met before it supported any proposals for a third runway. Consequently the government ruled out a full-length third runway, favouring instead a 2,000-metre (6,600-foot) runway to the north of the existing airport, suitable for use only by short-haul aircraft; and this provided that targets on aircraft noise, public transport and pollution could be met. In December 2006 the DfT published a progress report on the strategy, which confirmed the original vision. In November 2007 the government began a public consultation on its proposal for a third runway and a new passenger terminal.

In January 2009 the Transport Secretary, Geoff Hoon, announced that the UK government supported the expansion of Heathrow by building a longer third runway and a sixth terminal building. The Department for Transport stated: 'As the economic downturn demonstrates, we live in a global age. It is critical that Government makes the tough choices necessary to deliver long-term prosperity to the United Kingdom.'

With a change of government in May 2010, BAA, the airports operator, formally dropped plans for new runways at Heathrow on 24 May, bringing to a close one of the most controversial parts of the last Labour government's transport policy.

Heathrow handles sixty-eight million passengers a year, and it is an essential component of the UK economy. Still Europe's and the world's dominant international airport hub, with the continued introduction of very-long-range aircraft, this position is likely to be eroded in terms of it being a technical halt between India, Asia and North America. For every major international destination, Heathrow leads its European rivals with ease, with more flights per week to New York than the Amsterdam-Schiphol, Paris-Charles de Gaulle and Frankfurt operations combined. However, in terms of transfer passengers, Frankfurt has been in front for some years, and continues to be so. The BAA view is that while Heathrow Airport will grow to eighty-five million-plus passengers by 2015, the transfer number will remain fairly static at around twenty-two to twenty-three million.

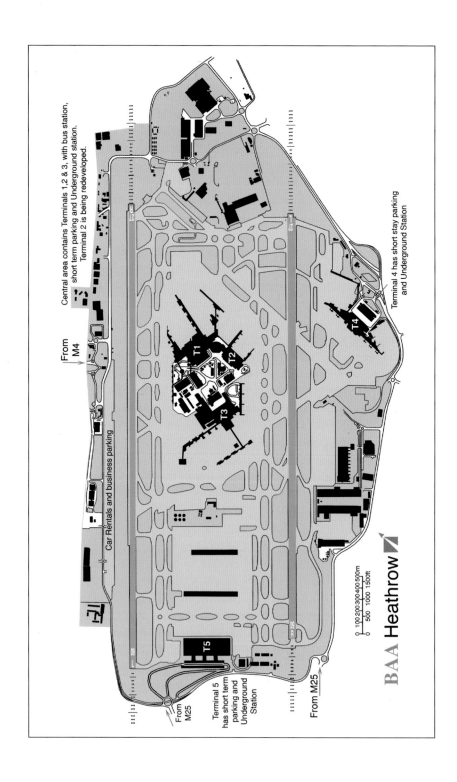

Central area contains Terminals 1,2 & 3, with bus station, short term parking and Underground station. Terminal 2 is being redeveloped.

Terminal 4 has short stay parking and Underground Station

From M4

Car Rentals and business parking

T1

T2

T3

T4

T5

From M25

Terminal 5 has short term parking and Underground Station

From M25

BAA Heathrow

0 100 200 300 400 500m
0   500 1000 1500ft

CHAPTER THREE

London City

The creation of an airport close to the centre of London was first proposed in 1981 by Reg Ward, the chief executive of the then newly formed London Docklands Development Corporation (LDDC), which was responsible for the regeneration of the area. He in turn discussed the proposal with Sir Philip Beck, the chairman of John Mowlem & Co. plc. From these talks emerged the concept of an international airport primarily for the use of business travellers. With its close proximity to the financial centre of the City of London, it was expected to prove very popular. Around the 'Royal' docks to the east of the Isle of Dogs lay a huge area of land suitable for redevelopment. The quay that stretched between the Albert and King George V Docks offered an ideal base for the suggested short runway. By November of that year Mowlems and Brymon Airways – a UK airline that specialised in operating Short Take-Off and Landing (STOL) aircraft – had submitted an outline proposal to the LDDC for a

An Air UK BAe 146: an example of the short take-off and landing aircraft that are allowed to use this small airport in the heart of London.

Docklands STOLport city-centre gateway. Mowlem began discussions with the landowner, resulting in an agreement being reached in 1983. An option on the land was secured while both design and financial implications were developed, pending a firm decision on investment in the project.

On 27 June 1982 Brymon Airways' Captain Harry Gee landed a de Havilland Canada Dash-7 on Heron Quays, in the West India Docks nearby, to demonstrate the feasibility of the STOLport project. This was a simple, highly practical method of convincing public and politicians alike that no harm could come to the environment if an airport became a feature of the East End of London. A study of potential passengers revealed that there was a strong demand, and later that year the LDDC published a feasibility study. An opinion poll among local residents showed the majority were in favour of the development of the airport. In 1983 Mowlem submitted the application for planning permission, which, after much discussion, was granted early in 1986. First to go were the derelict concrete-framed warehouses, but the discovery of asbestos necessitated great care during its removal and the need to maintain a strict monitoring programme for the rest of the clearance. The size of the airport was constrained by water-filled Royal Albert and King George V docks to the north and south respectively, which meant that there would be no covered maintenance facilities for aircraft. These had to be filled. The pair of docks associated with the Royal Albert were filled without problem, but the 820 × 100 ft dock at the end of the King George V could not be dealt with in this manner because the apron in front of the proposed terminal would cover the dock, and soil would settle as time progressed. A temporary dam was built to allow the dock to be pumped dry before the task of erecting 128 columns in two rows to support the steel beams carrying the concrete deck forming the apron area could begin. With this in place the old dock was once again flooded, to provide increased stability for the walls. Ventilation prevented any build-up of gases above the water level.

The 488-foot-wide quay between the two Royal docks, which conveniently pointed in the direction of the prevailing wind, provided the base and the required safety margins for the 3,379 ft runway, although the displaced thresholds dictate a declared length for both 10 and 28 of 2,500 feet. At the eastern end, a turning-circle of 197 ft diameter was laid, together with a pair of taxiways opposite the apron. There was insufficient room to build a parallel track, but with the number of movements planned this was not expected to prove a handicap. Also, the flight path would restrict the maximum height of new skyscrapers that could be built in and around Canary Wharf. To aid aircraft braking and tyre grip, a rough finish was applied to the surface of the runway, which was completed in readiness for the first Dash-7 landing on 31 May 1987. This honour was bestowed upon Brymon, the carrier that had supported the project throughout, but the inaugural take-off was made by a Eurocity Express aircraft. HRH Prince Charles laid the foundation stone of the terminal building on 29 May 1986. On 26 October 1987 a Brymon Dash-7 landed at London City at 07.30 hours, to become the first revenue-earning movement at the airport. Virtually a transit stop, it departed thirty-five minutes later, bound for Paris-Charles de Gaulle. Queen Elizabeth II officially opened London City Airport in November of the same year.

Placing a commercial airport into the congested airspace of the London Terminal Area zone was a challenge for the National Air Traffic Services, and a new airspace authority, Thames Radar, was established to provide a radar control service and provide safe separations for London City arrivals and departures. In 1988, the first full year of operation, the airport handled 133,000 passengers. The earliest scheduled destinations were Plymouth, Paris, Amsterdam and Rotterdam. With a runway of only 1,080 metres (3,543 feet) in length, and a glideslope of seven and a half degrees for noise abatement purposes, the airport could only be

London City Airport in 1996.

With rear airbrake extended, a Lufthansa BAe 146 comes in to land.

London City Airport's main runway as seen from the control tower.

The famous London docklands in the background as this BAe 146 climbs out after take-off. The airport's close proximity to Canary Wharf and the tent-like O2 centre, formally the Millennium Dome, can be clearly observed.

A British Airways aircraft climbs away after take-off. The Docklands Light Railway Station in the foreground.

used by a very limited number of aircraft types – principally the Dash-7 and the smaller Dornier Do 228. In 1989 the airport submitted a planning application to extend the runway, allowing the use of a larger number of aircraft types. By 1990 passengers figures doubled to 230,000, but the figures fell drastically during the Gulf War and did not recover until 1993, when 245,000 passengers were carried. By this time the extended runway had been opened on 5 March 1992. At the same time the glideslope was reduced to five and a half degrees, still steep for a European airport, but sufficient to allow a larger range of aircraft, including the BAe 146 regional jet to serve the airport. By 1995 passenger numbers reached the half million, and Mowlem sold the airport to Irish businessman Dermot Desmond. Five years later, passenger numbers had climbed to 1,580,000 and over 30,000 flights were operated. By 2006 more than 2.3 million passengers used the airport.

On 2 December 2005 London City Airport Docklands Light Railway station was opened, providing rail access to the airport for the first time, and fast rail links to Canary Wharf and the City of London. On 30 November of that year, the airport was sold again, this time to a consortium consisting of insurer AIG and Global Infrastructure Partners. In 2001 planning permission was granted allowing construction of an extended apron on piles above the water of the King George V Dock, with four additional aircraft parking stands and four new gates to the east of the terminal. These became operational on 30 May 2008.

The airport's stringent rules on noise levels from aircraft operations (helicopters are denied access for environmental reasons), together with the physical dimensions of the 1,508-metre (4,948-foot) long runway and the steep glideslope, limits the aircraft types that can use London City. Corporate aircraft such as the Beechcraft Super King Air, Cessna Citation Jet series, Hawker 400 and 800, Piaggio Avanti and variants of the Dassault Falcon business jets are increasingly common. Mid-range airliners seen include the ATR 42 and 72, Airbus A318, DHC Dash-8, BAe 146, Dornier 328, Embraer ERJ 135 and 170 and Fokker 50. In 2006 successful compatibility testing for the A318 was undertaken. In 2009 the ATR72-500 and the Embraer 190SR successfully completed trials and were approved for operation at the airport.

On 29 September 2009 British Airways commenced its transatlantic service via Shannon, in Ireland, to JFK International Airport in New York, with Airbus A318s configured for just thirty-two passengers in Club World 'flat-bed' seats. With a full load of fuel, the A318's take-off roll would be too long for London

City's runway. At Shannon the 318s are refuelled for a non-stop flight to Kennedy. Because of this stopover and the slightly lower cruising speed compared to other transatlantic airliners, the trip from London to New York takes ninety minutes more than a comparable flight from Heathrow, but with unprecedented luxury. The service has revived the prestigious BA001, 002, 003 and 004 flight numbers previously used for Concorde operations.

The size and layout of London City, and the overall complexity caused by the lack of taxiways, means that the airport is very busy during peak hours. The air traffic controllers have to deal with over thirty-eight flights an hour on a runway requiring a time-consuming backtrack for each aircraft needing to depart from Runway 27 or land on Runway 09. In 2003 a new holding-point was established at the eastern end of the runway, enabling aircraft awaiting take-off to hold while other aircraft landed. Operations are restricted to 06.30 to 22.00 Monday to Friday, 06.30 to 12.30 on Saturdays, and 12.30 to 22.00 on Sundays, which gives residents some relief from noise.

In 2002 a private jet centre catering for corporate aviation was opened, as well as additional aircraft stands at the western end of the apron, making London City the closest 'biz-jet' centre to central London. In 2005 it was voted the best corporate aviation passenger-handling facility in Europe by *European Business Air News*. Unlike most of the smaller airports, London City is at its busiest during the winter months, when a number of airlines, most notably Swiss International and CityJet, fly to ski resort gateway destinations. Zurich, Geneva, Strasbourg and Milan are among the destinations popular among winter sports enthusiasts. In January 2010 London City Airport had twelve airlines serving twenty-nine destinations across the UK and Europe, and connections to the rest of the world through major European hubs, and it was starting to market itself in connection with the 2012 Olympic Games. It boasts the lowest check-in times compared to any other airport in London. Airlines offer a twenty-minute check-in time for passengers with hand luggage, and a minimum of thirty for those with hold luggage. A 'no-queues' policy means the average time for a passenger to process security takes two minutes. Security queues are constantly monitored for customer-satisfaction purposes. Early in 2010 the headlines 'Majorca from the East End' appeared. It seems that Majorca in the Spanish Balearic islands was to gain a new UK route for the summer season from the most unlikely of airports. After dropping Barcelona, British Airways is to introduce a London City route to Palma in May, operating an Embraer 190. Probably the first pure leisure service

London City Airport.

British Airways now operate a scheduled service to New York from the heart of London with the Airbus A-318.

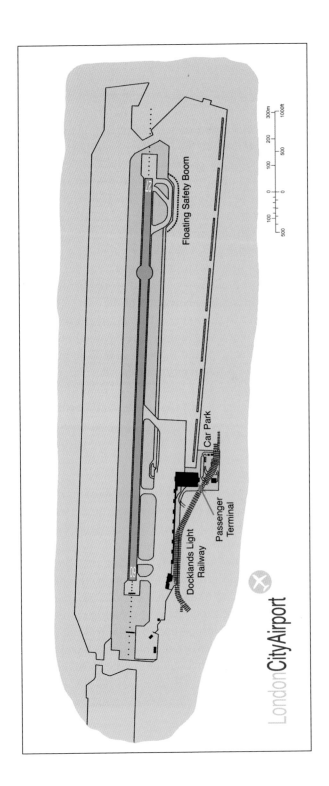

Floating Safety Boom

Car Park

Passenger
Terminal

Docklands Light
Railway

London City Airport

17

09

300m
1000ft

200

100

0
0

100

500

500

from the airport, it operated initially on a three-times-a-week basis, Fridays, Sundays and Mondays.

Long seen as a major hub for business travellers, due to its proximity to London's Docklands and financial district, the number of leisure travellers has also begun to increase, probably because of increasing congestion at other airports. An application to extend the number of flights from 80,000 to 120,000 per annum was made in a response to the White Paper 'The Future of Air Transport', which required airport operators to maximise the use of existing runways. London City Airport's master plan outlining its vision for growth shows a phased expansion of the airport, giving the capability of handling eight million passengers per annum by 2030, but it does not propose the addition of a second runway or significant expansion of the airport boundaries. Phase 1 would be undertaken by 2015. It would include the in-progress construction of the eastern apron extension and provision of a finger pier to the south of this apron to provide passenger access to aircraft using the new parking stands. The terminal building would also be extended to use the triangle of land between it and the railway station. The jet centre would be extended, a new hangar built to allow aircraft maintenance, and a replacement fire station provided. Phases 2 and 3 would be undertaken between 2015 and 2030. Further aircraft parking stands would be built to the east of the terminal, and a taxiway would be constructed alongside and to the south of the runway, to avoid the need for aircraft to back-track on the runway. Both these developments would involve further reduction in the water area of the King George V Dock. The existing fuel farm would be relocated to a site at the east of the airport, where it could be supplied by barge and linked to a hydrant-based supply system, thus eliminating both road tanker deliveries and on-airport fuel bowser movements. The existing surface car park would be replaced by a multi-storey car park, allowing extension of the vehicle drop-off and pick-up area.

An inspector's report was submitted, declaring that the planned expansion was fully justified and could go ahead. One concern highlighted in the report was the expected rise in noise levels that the additional traffic would cause, but around a thousand jobs were expected to be created as a result of the expansion. Accessibility to the airport is also expected to increase in the near future with the approval of the $16 billion Crossrail project, which will improve access from central London and will service five stations in the Newham area.

CHAPTER FOUR

Luton

Luton Airport dates back to the early 1930s, when Alan Cobham, who was widely respected as being one of the greatest aerodrome consultants of his day, became the founding director of National Flying Services Ltd – an organisation created to co-ordinate the increasing number of flying clubs that were being formed around the country. Before offering his services to Luton Corporation, the arch-propagandist for British aviation had set off on a tour of over one hundred towns and cities in the UK with a simple aim – to impress upon local dignitaries that there was a need for municipal aerodromes. At Luton a number of sites were made available, the most promising being Eaton Green Farm, which was offered in 1935. It was just over 300 acres and was only two and a half miles from the town centre. In March 1937 flying commenced from what was still an unlicensed aerodrome. Mr H.T. Rushton, who had been the assistant airport manager and control officer at Liverpool, was appointed aerodrome manager. 'Facilities' were either improved or put into place to make it habitable, and the farmhouse was modified to create office accommodation. Plans were drafted for a terminal building to include administration offices and customs facilities. The Airport Committee also considered a modern administration building housing a new control tower, wireless station and meteorological offices, as well as being something of a social centre, with a spectator balcony, hotel, restaurant and even a dance hall, all with a superb view over the apron. It was thought that Luton should to be designated the Northern Terminal for London, so that air travellers from Scotland, Northern Ireland and the north of England would not have to land at Croydon. To aid identification, the word 'LUTON' was carved into the turf in letters that could be read on approach from up to 4,000 feet.

The aerodrome was officially opened on 16 July 1938, but with the outbreak of war progress was slowed. After the war it seemed likely that Luton would be a very

A BAC 1-11 at Luton in the early 1970s.

successful commercial concern, with an extended aerodrome and four additional hangars. Additional land and buildings were purchased, and Hunting set up a base to begin air charter operations by ordering a fleet of Percival Proctors from Percival Aircraft. Hunting Air Travel also became dealers for the range of Percival aircraft, and on 1 January 1946, one of Hunting's Proctors had the distinction of making the first post-war air taxi flight in the British Isles. In January 1947, in line with its expansion programme, Hunting Air Travel opened new offices at Pall Mall in London. The following month Hunting moved its main operations base to Gatwick, and another base was established at Nottingham, partly because of the continued lack of customs facilities at Luton. In time customs facilities enabled operations direct to the continent, and led to a natural growth in the use of the aerodrome. The Lady Mayor and Chairman of the Airport Committee in

The control tower at Luton Airport.

1947 said that Luton should '... seize the opportunity to advance towards an airport worthy of such original vision, commensurate with the industrial importance of the Borough'. On 1 April 1950 Harold Bamberg's Eagle Aviation moved its operation to Luton from Aldermaston, bringing with it a Handley Page Halifax and a number of Avro Yorks purchased from BOAC. Eagle was only based at Luton for a short time, for in November Bamberg bought the Blackbushe-based Aviation Servicing, and moved his maintenance and operations facility to that airfield. In September 1950 the Airport Committee decided it would build a new control tower on the north side of the aerodrome, and in the following year the aerodrome was granted a one-year trial of customs facilities. At last, Luton had an airport. On 25 October 1951 the new Conservative government brought about a change of policy regarding independent charter operators, and new regulations allowed Inclusive Tour (IT) Holidays by air at an inclusive price. Licences for inclusive tour flights were issued on a seasonal basis, but renewal was not automatic.

On 27 February 1952 the future arrived unexpectedly at Luton when a de Havilland Comet 1, the world's first commercial jet airliner, made an unscheduled landing at Luton when its base at Hatfield Aerodrome became smog-bound. Test pilot Group Captain John Cunningham landed and took off from Luton without problems – even on Luton's grass runways. The new control tower was opened in September by the Minister of Transport and Civil Aviation, who promised that the airport would receive as much Ministry help as possible to forward development. At the same time, Autair, a helicopter charter company founded by William 'Bill' Armstrong, was established at Luton. This company not only roamed the world with its heli-ops, but would become a long-term Luton operator and play a very important part in the airport's development. Autair need a fixed-wing operation to support its heli-ops, and so Armstrong created Autair International. The ad hoc operation rapidly expanded into an airline, firstly operating DC-3s, and later, Vickers Vikings and Airspeed Ambassadors. In 1957 McAlpine Aviation moved its base to a hangar on the north side of the airport. There were more newcomers like Luton Airways and Pegasus Airlines, and by the end of 1958 the first freight operation was up and running when Vauxhall cars and spare parts were ferried to Ireland in a BKS Bristol Freighter. These were followed by the launch of Derby Airways' scheduled service between Luton and Jersey with a DC-3 Dakota.

In May 1959 the Mayor, Alderman Mrs F.M. Brash, blew a whistle and sounded a klaxon that started construction of Luton's new concrete runway. Luton also planned for a large hangar and a new terminal building, which would house airline offices, freight sheds and the customs office. Originally, the terminal was to be rather basic in design, but would allow conversion to alternative usage when the proper terminal was completed. Although the customs facility had been withdrawn, it was reinstated on a trial basis. A conference took as its theme the subject of 'Air Charter Passenger and Freight Traffic'. The airport's catchment area had a thirty-mile radius, plus the south Midlands – more if the new M1 motorway was a success – and embraced a population of four million people. It was stressed that Luton should be developed by the independent airlines for charter, inclusive tours, vehicle ferrying and private executive travel. Many of the local businesses had still to realise the potential of having an airport on their doorstep. At this conference, the airport disclosed its five-year plan, including a 5,000 ft north–south runway, a permanent terminal building with shops, bank and public enclosure, further hangars and additional apronage.

During the next ten years, 'package holidays' allowed many people to travel abroad for the first time. Luton played an important role in the development of this business in the UK. Euravia (London) Ltd was formed in 1962 as a charter airline to carry its Universal Sky Tours passengers on inclusive tour holidays to the Mediterranean, using three ex-El Al Lockheed Constellations in eighty-two-seat configuration. The new airline anticipated handling 700 holiday flights during 1962, and agreed to base its aircraft at Luton on the condition that passenger amenities were increased. As a result, the terminal building was almost doubled in size between January and April, and Euravia also leased a quarter of the new corporation hangar (about 12,000 square feet, or 1,115 square metres), which allowed the airline much-needed workshop space, stores and offices. Soon, Euravia was processing almost 250 passengers each morning and evening. The terminal was bulging with even more passengers during the high season, as Derby Airways and Autair routed their own traffic through. On 16 August 1964 Euravia became Britannia Airways, named after its new aircraft (ex-BOAC 112-seat Bristol Britannias), and the next year it became part of the Canadian-owned International Thomson Organisation.

Because of the increase in air traffic, Luton started to monitor aircraft departure and arrival noise levels. The village of Caddington, three miles to the west, was suffering most, and so from September 1963 departing traffic made a twenty-degree left turn after take-off to avoid the village. The airport formulated a five-year plan, which included improved access, a north–south concrete runway, the

Two independent airlines operated out of Luton at the end of the last century.

first phase of the new terminal building, twenty-nine stands for aircraft up to Comet size and a heliport. In 1964, despite the complaints from the anti-airport campaigners in local villages, extension work to the runway commenced to bring it up from 5,432 to 6,600 feet. In 1963/4 there had been an alarming increase in the number of noise-related complaints from residents of the surrounding villages, and in October 1964 they formed an Action Group. At an inquiry at the Town Hall in November, residents expressed their fears over the runway extension, but an expert study concluded that this would not result in any significant increase in the levels of landing and take-off noise.

Britannia intended to continue Luton operations for at least the next five years, and a permanent terminal building came into use in 1966, but ever-increasing passenger numbers soon placed a strain on the building, and so the airport committee proceeded with plans for major improvements to meet the demands of the peak season. Redevelopment work costing over £700,000 included a new passenger lounge, shops, customs hall, immigration area, apron extension, a new approach road and parking for 450 cars. The terminal building was three times the capacity of its predecessor, but still easily converted to alternative use at a later date. Luton also received ministry approval to make a further extension to the runway on the grounds that there would be little discernible increase in noise and runway operations would be safer.

The terminal building was well under way, and a licence was issued that allowed passengers to purchase alcoholic drinks during normal hours. The restriction on hours was lifted when Luton was officially designated an international airport. This was a blessing to Autair passengers, as the airline had just opened its north London terminal in Finchley, where passengers were able to take a coach transfer to Luton. British Midland Airways' newly launched Channel Islands route was a huge success, resulting in the company turning passengers away, but additional flights were laid on for May, and the service was soon operating seven days a week. Also, Autair's successful Luton–Blackpool service was extended to include Glasgow. Towards the end of the year Luton was rejected as a candidate for becoming London's third airport because of the limitation in potential expansion and the inherent intrusion into Heathrow air space. Amid forecasts of passenger and aircraft increases in the next five years, plans were drawn up for an express road linking Luton airport with the M1. Passenger numbers were growing to the point where it was apparent that the new terminal would soon meet the same fate as the one it had just replaced, as projections for 1967 estimated that 350,000 passengers would be using the airport. Luton also applied to the Board of Trade to have its named changed to 'Luton Airport (London)', thus reflecting its true geographical position.

Monarch Airlines was formed on 5 June 1967 as a subsidiary of Globus Gateway Holdings, which was also the owner of the UK-based tour operator Cosmos Tours. Monarch chose Luton as a base, and commenced commercial airline operations on 5 April 1968 with a charter flight from Luton to Madrid using a pair of Bristol Britannias. The airline established a London terminal in Tottenham Court Road and was already contemplating its third Britannia for delivery in 1968. This was the time of rapid expansion in the package tour business, and by 1969 a fifth of all holiday flights from the UK departed from Luton Airport. By 1972 Luton had become Britain's most profitable airport.

Britannia Airways was about to enter the Jet Age with an order for Boeing 737s in a deal worth £6 million, and Autair allocated £3 million to two BAC 1-11 400s. At the turn of the year, Britannia began work on a new hangar in a construction contract valued at £750,000. Halcyon Breeze, the first of Autair's 1-11s, was delivered in February 1968, and soon afterwards the airline started a twice-daily scheduled service to Dundee, using a Handley Page Herald. In 1968 there were thirteen Luton-based night flights each week, a number of them being jet services. Parish, local and county councils banded together to jointly commission a consultant noise expert to help fight the proposed future development of Luton. Dan-Air had applied for, but was denied, permission to operate from Luton because of terminal overcrowding, but permission from Whitehall to enlarge the terminal was found unnecessary, and it was modified to accommodate the airline's expected 2,500 movements, and permission granted to operate from the airport. The 1969 summer season was a holidaymaker's nightmare, with delays caused by industrial action from foreign air traffic controllers. Flights to Spain were held back by up to six hours. At that time, there were thirty-eight night flights each week and an increase in jet traffic, and so monitoring of noise levels was reintroduced. In 1970 throughput was estimated at two and a quarter million passengers, and so night flights were increased to ten each day. A residents' petition expressed 'total dissatisfaction' with the airport, and local travel agents formed APLANE – the Association for Promotion of Luton Airport Natural Expansion to support the enterprise.

The new decade saw bright new colours at Luton, with Autair's name changed to Court Line. Court's eight BAC One-Eleven jets were painted in vivid colours borrowed from sunsets and holiday beaches with silver highlights, and titling with uniforms designed by husband-and-wife team Peter and Julia Murdoch to match. Monarch, meanwhile was considering its requirement for the early 1970s, and examined the possible use of Boeing 720s and 727s and Trident 2Es. They eventually opted for the powerful 720B. Britannia meanwhile leased a pair of Boeing 707s. Court Line ordered a further three 1-11s in June 1970. With more jets for residents to worry about and, when the weather became extremely hot that summer, pilots of jet-engined aircraft finding it necessary to use more than the normal degree of thrust to climb away, more noise complaints were received. Luton was having enormous difficulty winning friends. After yet another change of flight path, this time by the Board of Trade, Hertfordshire County Council demanded that the Secretary of State for Trade and Industry impose greater limits on aircraft movements.

Although there had been plans for a £1.5 million development programme, the airport committee opted for a £2.5 million alternative, which would enable Luton to handle larger aircraft, thus increasing revenue and passenger throughput and at the same time giving a reduction in night flights. The government responded by establishing a public inquiry. The airport committee considered levying a 'noise tax' on the carriers, and linked it with a plan to surcharge in the form of a peak-time landing-charge. Court Line decided almost immediately that it would relinquish its 1-11s for much quieter aircraft. Invicta International Airways doubled its nights through Luton and increased its fleet to four Vickers Vanguards. Dan-Air inaugurated its Luton–Leeds–Glasgow scheduled service in April 1972. As the summer became hotter, so did the noise debate, which resulted in a reduction in night flights by 1,000. A public inquiry attracted representation from fifty organisations vehemently against development of the airport. The government said it was crucial that Luton should continue as a major airport until at least 1980. Development should not lead to increased movements, but allow the handling of larger aircraft with a greater capacity for passengers. It was expecting ten TriStars to be operative from Luton by the end of 1976, and a reduction in the movement of medium-sized, noisier jet aircraft. Court Line realised that it needed to increase capacity, and arranged for the Lockheed L.1101 TriStar demonstrator visiting the 1972 Farnborough Air Show to fly to Luton for viewing. With a seat configuration of more than three times the passenger capacity of a 1-11, it was an impressive aircraft. Local action groups, too, were impressed by the quietness of the TriStar. Court Line placed an order for two

TriStars, with options on more. Halcyon Days, its first L.1101, arrived in March 1973, the second arriving two months later.

Meanwhile, two tented areas were erected to relieve departure lounge congestion at peak periods. At times, the marquees were handling 2,000 passengers an hour, with airport personnel working hard to keep the area clean and tidy, but fears were expressed that the airport was likely to win itself a 'slum' image from customers. Tour operators stated that the UK's largest air travel market had been built up at Luton by popular demand and that the government's attitude was likely to dissuade passengers from using Luton, never to return. A ministerial decision decided that planning approval for Luton Airport was appropriate, but there would be temporary accommodation alongside the existing terminal building while a two-storey extension was built.

The airport management pointed out that the prime objective was to ensure profitability, and this required expansion to allow an even greater number of air travellers to enjoy the facilities. It feared that a refusal for Luton's expansion plans would sound alarms with those carriers and businesses already based at the airport and that they were likely to move out. A noise consultant put the case that larger aircraft would mean some increase in environmental noise by 1976, but to retain medium-sized jet aircraft of the type being used at the time would be an environmental disaster as far as local towns and villages were concerned. A conservative estimate placed a further 100,000 people under threat of possible noise nuisance. However, the cause of a number of the complaints originated, not from Luton, but from Heathrow air traffic. In January 1973 the Environment Minister announced that there would be no development of Luton, but the government finally approved three phases of development at the onset of 1974.

The first phase was a prefabricated terminal extension, the second a two-storey terminal building of 1,115 square metres (20,000 square feet), and finally an extension to the arrivals hall with an improved departure lounge. In return Luton agreed to a 10.2% reduction in night movements for 1974, with more decreases to be instigated later. But then airlines began moving their flights out of Luton and operating their larger programmes from other airports. Court Line voted to remain at Luton, but began moving more flights to Gatwick. Shortly afterwards, Britannia announced that it was pulling out of the long-haul market. And then an oil crisis began on 15 October 1973 when the Organization of Arab Petroleum Exporting Countries (OPEC) announced an oil embargo.

By 1974 Clarksons, Court Line's main customer, was facing mounting financial pressure, and Horizon Holidays collapsed. Court Line purchased Clarksons to prevent its liquidation, and in a desperate attempt to fill the group's aircraft and hotel rooms, began selling its holiday packages below cost. The inevitable happened – on 16 August Court Line collapsed, leaving thousands of holidaymakers stranded at Luton and abroad. Despite the economic crisis, the British air travelling public appeared to regard a sun-soaked holiday as the best possible pick-me-up, and bookings were up 250% at the beginning of 1975. Britannia and Monarch, meanwhile, were showing steady growth, and by the middle of the year Global Holidays announced that it was to expand its use of Luton. By 1976 Monarch had become an all-jet fleet following the retirement of the last remaining Britannias. By 1977 Luton was doing more than other airports to be a good neighbour, and had invested in the latest noise-monitoring equipment. Pilots could now be notified of their noise rating direct from the control tower. But still many residents were adamantly opposed to the airport's development. A 1978 Government White Paper, stating that Luton was an integral part of the London airports system, fulfilling an important role, also made the point that noise from Luton traffic affected fewer residents than that of the other major airports in the London area.

The airport committee began the preparation of a master plan to take Luton Airport into the 1990s and on to five million passengers. Soon after the planning was under way, the airport heard that Horizon was planning to feed 30,000 passengers through Luton, and Ellermans a further 40,000 passengers, during 1979. The first two months of 1979 brought welcome news to the airport. Cosmos had set up a 30,000-passenger programme through Luton, using off-peak departures and arrivals. The new programme – called Late Night Specials – was to operate throughout the season, April to October. The annual reports showed that Luton had started to recover from the collapse of Court Line. Gross profits stood at over £2 million, aircraft movements 62,000, and more than 7,000 tons of freight. All were new record figures for Luton. This resulted in the third successive year where airport profits allowed substantial reductions in the Luton rates bill – a point seemingly lost on the noise complainers! In April, Horizon was off with a fine start and its 36,000-passenger programme – and the next month, two new airlines launched services from Luton. Royal Air Maroc had a launch in party mood for its inauguration of a weekly service to Tangiers, and the Yugoslavian national carrier, JAT, celebrated its first Luton departure by using President Tito's personal aircraft.

In 1981 Monarch Airlines became launch customer for four 757-200 high-capacity, medium-haul airliners powered by new-technology Rolls-Royce RB211-535C engines. Monarch was the first charter airline in the UK, as well as the rest of Europe, to order the Boeing 757. Monarch's first 757s were delivered and entered commercial airline service during spring 1983. Two years later Britannia became the first European airline to operate the Boeing 767, and a £5 million hangar was built so that maintenance work could be carried out. The first stage of a new terminal building costing £8 million was opened with airline offices at first-floor level above the covered passenger set-down area to allow the necessary facilities and levels of comfort for three and a half million passengers. By the late summer, it was evident that overall passenger throughput was decreasing, although the airport had only recently given its thirty-millionth passenger a champagne send-off. But even with reduced profits and the condition that Monarch and Britannia fund the construction of their own hangarage for their 757 and 767 jets respectively, the Airport Committee elected to proceed with Phases 2 and 3 of the terminal. Passengers were still using Luton at a rate of two million a year. Duty-free goods had only been obtainable on board aircraft, but in 1984 the airport management decided that it was time for Luton, the only major UK international airport still without a duty-free retail facility, to have its own duty-free shop.

The public inquiry on the future of Stansted concluded that the airport should be developed to accommodate a target throughput of fifteen million passengers, but that Luton should continue as a major gateway airport, it and was recognised as being of local and national importance as a departure point. At the height of the 1985 season, buoyed by the news that Monarch had been given CAA approval to launch scheduled services to Palma, Malaga and Menorca, a Government White Paper approved Luton's advance towards five million passengers in 1990. On 11 July HRH Prince Charles arrived by helicopter to open the new terminal building, the culmination of five years of building works by the construction group John Laing. In 1986 Monarch Crown Service began scheduled flights to Spain, and Ryanair launched scheduled services to Ireland to mark the growth of scheduled air services from Luton. Ryanair, which had been operating out of Gatwick for eight months prior to its move to Luton, began twenty-five return flights to Dublin every week and six flights to Waterford. Both routes featured an unrestricted, attractively priced fare. Founded in 1985 by Adam 'Ryan' Cooke, Liam Lonergan (owner of an Irish tour operator, Club Travel) and noted Irish businessman Tony Ryan, founder of Guinness Peat Aviation, the airline began with a fifteen-seat Embraer Bandeirante turboprop aircraft flying between Waterford and Gatwick, with the aim of breaking the duopoly on London–Ireland flights, at that time held by British Airways and Aer Lingus. In 1986 the company added a second route – flying Dublin–London Luton in direct competition with Aer Lingus and BA. With two routes and two aircraft, the fledgling airline carried 82,000 passengers in one year. Passenger numbers continued to increase, but the airline generally ran at a loss, and by 1991 it was in need of restructuring, and Michael O'Leary was charged with the task of making the airline profitable. O'Leary visited the USA to study the 'low fares/no frills' model being used by Southwest Airlines, and he quickly decided that the key to low fares was to implement quick turn-around times for aircraft, 'no frills' and no business class, as well as operating a single model of aircraft. O'Leary was convinced that Ryanair could make huge inroads into the European air market by providing a low-cost service. Flights were scheduled into regional airports, which offered lower landing and handling charges than larger, established, international airports. Ryanair's popularity grew rapidly, as did its services. Very quickly, the company was looking to secure jets for its routes, later acquiring leased RomBAC 1-11s. At the close of September, Ryanair's 50,000th passenger passed through the terminal. Approval of the jet aircraft operations came in October 1986, more than doubling capacity on the Luton–Dublin route and reducing journey time to fifty-five minutes.

In 1987 Luton International Airport became a limited company, with Luton Borough Council as sole shareholder. The airport was renamed London Luton Airport in 1990 to mark its position as part of the London airport network, but a decline in passenger numbers struck again in 1991, as Ryanair moved a large part of its business to Stansted. But the M25 London orbital motorway was nearing completion early in 1986, bringing Luton within reach of larger numbers of potential passengers who would make the airport more attractive to scheduled service operators. The 'Luton Flyer' rail/coach link was launched to meet air travellers at Luton Railway Station and speed them straight to the airport, dropping them right outside the terminal building. Such easy access proved of benefit to families flying abroad on holiday, and the airport introduced a new crèche facility.

In August 1988 the Thomson Travel Group purchased Horizon Travel and its airline, Orion Airways, which was integrated into Britannia. A period of steady

Ryanair is now one of the world's most successful airlines. Its no-frills approach to air travel appeals to many travellers. Luton is one of the Irish airline's bases. easyJet is also one of Britain's favourite holiday and short-haul airlines and frequents Luton on many occasions.

expansion at Luton followed until the emergence of easyJet Airline Company Ltd, which was launched by Stelios Haji-Ioannou on 18 October 1995. This airline started operations on 10 November that year with two wet-leased Boeing 737-200s, and it grew into one of the largest low-fare airlines in Europe, operating domestic and international scheduled services. easyJet became well known, in part due to the docu-soap series *Airline* on TV, which followed the airline's operations at Luton and later at a number of other bases. easyJet has seen rapid expansion, having grown through a combination of acquisitions and base openings fuelled by consumer demand for low-cost air travel.

In 1991 an unsuccessful attempt was made to sell Luton airport, and a new management team was appointed to stop the losses and improve passenger numbers. Over the next five years £30 million was invested in the airport infrastructure, and facilities were significantly improved. These upgraded facilities included a new air traffic control tower, new cargo centre, the extension and refurbishment of the passenger terminal, new access road, extension of the car parking adjacent to the passenger terminal and the installation of a Category 3 instrument landing

system. Passenger levels increased rapidly,with 3.4 million in 1997/8, and rising again to 4.4 million by 1998/9, making London Luton the UK's fastest-growing major airport.

With easy access from the London conurbation, Luton has established itself as one of the UK's main centres for business aviation. Harrods Aviation and Signature Flight Support are the main providers of the airport's extensive support services. In order to expand further, London Luton Airport signed a unique private-public partnership in 1998 to secure financial investment for the future. This meant the airport remained publicly owned by Luton Borough Council but was to be managed and developed by a new private consortium. An £80 million development programme was completed in autumn 1999, giving the airport a £40 million terminal with sixty check-in desks, modern baggage and flight information systems and a range of shops, restaurants and bars. The distinctively styled building faced the 1985 terminal, many of the functions of which it has replaced. Connecting the new terminal to the central core severed the previous road access to the airport, completing the reorientation of traffic towards the south-west. Also, the airport's parallel taxiway was extended; new, widened aircraft stands were constructed, the taxiway linking the runway and east apron was improved, and car park facilities were upgraded. The tunnel incorporates space for a people-mover/tramway connection with Luton Airport Parkway Railway Station, about a mile distant, which makes the journey to central London less than thirty minutes. A new freight facility and control tower, improved access via the short tunnel under a taxiway, and better road connections towards the M1 were also built. The project also created more departure gates, aircraft stands with repositioned customs and immigration. More operational flexibility resulted from the completion of a circuit of the central area by taxiways.

In November 1999 the passenger terminal was officially opened by HM The Queen and HRH The Duke of Edinburgh, who made the thirty-five-minute train journey to Luton airport from London's Moorgate Station. The terminal was refurbished further in 2000 with improvements to the departures and arrivals area, baggage reclaim facilities and new retail and catering outlets. In 2001 6.3 million passengers passed through the terminal, and this figure continued to grow as the demand for inclusive/package holidays increased at the UK's seventh-largest airport. In July 2005 the upper storey became the main airside lounge and retail/catering area.

Luton has a number of fixed base operators (FBOs), which are usually described as a service centre at an airport that may be a private enterprise or a department of the municipality that the airport serves. The term is originally North American, but it is becoming commoner in Europe and the UK. At a minimum, most FBOs offer aircraft fuel, oil and parking, along with access to washrooms and telephones. Some FBOs offer additional aircraft services, such as hangar (indoor) storage, maintenance, aircraft charter or rental, flight training, de-icing and ground services such as towing and baggage handling. One of those is Harrods Aviation, which provides a London-based business aviation service offering high-quality FBO services at London Luton and London Stansted airports. Both bases have fully equipped hangars for aircraft maintenance and engineering, where authorised service facility accreditations include Bombardier and Sikorsky.

Another business FBO at Luton is Signature Flight Support, which was founded in 1992 with the merger of two leading aviation service companies – Butler Aviation and Page Avjet Corporation. As with Harrods Aviation, which evolved from Fields Aircraft Services and Hunting Business Aviation, the current Signature company evolved from a number of other organisations. Today, Signature has grown to be the largest and most respected name in FBO services, with more than sixty years of experience in developing, operating and maintaining first-class facilities and providing first-class services at the world's leading commercial and general aviation airports. Just thirty miles from central London, Signature's London Luton FBO has consistently been voted best European FBO by the readers of *Professional Pilot* magazine.

The facility's one-stop, full service capability and world-class levels of service have ensured that it remains one of the busiest FBOs outside the USA, with in excess of 13,000 air traffic movements annually.

In contrast to the incremental changes over many years, in 2005 the operators announced a programme that would radically reshape, enlarge and reposition London Luton airport. In response to the 2003 White Paper, 'The Future of Air Transport', that identified a growth potential up to thirty million passengers a year by 2030 (it was eight million in 2003), the airport operator TBI published its master plan, costed at £1.5 billion, in October 2005. Its radical vision included a second runway – the current one being retained for taxiing and emergency use – being built to the south-east side of the existing perimeter, which would have pushed into farmland and small communities, also involving extensive

The check-in hall at Luton.

reshaping of the landscape. A new terminal and control tower also formed part of the plan, which was to powerfully reignite long-standing opposition to increased air traffic at Luton. This was most vocal around the rural eastern end of the airport that would be most affected by the development and ensuing aircraft movements. Unexpectedly, the operators announced on 6 July 2007 that in view of uncertainty over the scale of returns within the balance of their thirty-year tenure at Luton, the master plan was withdrawn.

Demetrio Ullastres, chairman of the London Luton Airport Operations Ltd, the parent company, said that they were 'committed to the delivery of facilities that meet the needs of our customers and at the same time fulfil our shareholder expectations. Therefore, we have decided that our proposals should focus on making the most of the existing airport site.' New development proposals were said to be forthcoming.

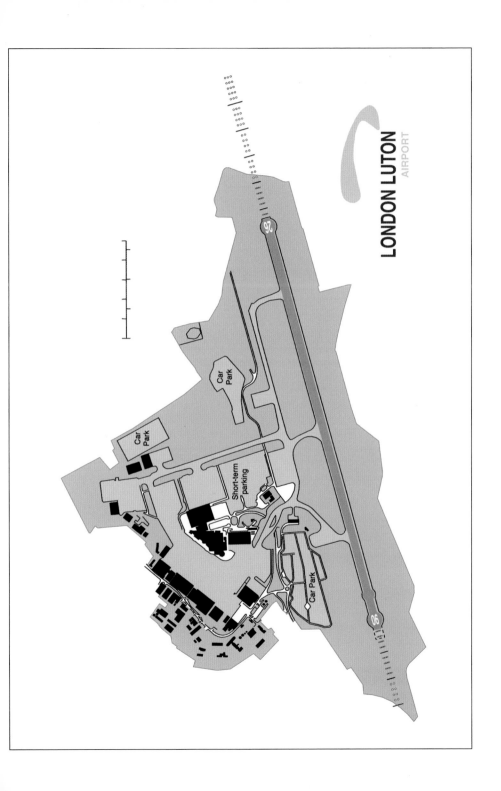

LONDON LUTON
AIRPORT

Car Park

Car Park

Short-term parking

Car Park

26

06

CHAPTER FIVE

Stansted

Next stop Nice

Passengers were probably settling down, reading, chatting and looking out of the cabin windows. Not even Sterling Service can compare with the First Class experience of a ring-side seat in the ultra-modern cockpit of a Fokker F100. Small boys of all ages would surely trade a place on the footplate of a steam engine or the snug fit of a racing-car for the third seat at the sharp end of the F100. On take-off the jump seat aboard G-UKFI provides an unparalleled view over the shoulders of the captain and first officer.

The long, grey Stansted runway tapers off into the distance like a flight simulator computer game. Two mighty Rolls-Royce Tay 620.15 turbofans, each with a static thrust of over 14,000 lb, propel us powerfully, almost effortlessly, into the murk over Essex like a piercing dart. The F100 is 116 feet long, has a 92 ft wingspan and, depending on the galley fit, is capable of seating between ninety-nine and 101 passengers in five-abreast configuration. There's no disguising the pleasure it gives the two pilots to know that they are leaving the mid-morning murk behind and heading for Nice in the south of France. The captain's first journey of the day was, like that taken by most captains of industry, heading for his hot seat in the city. It had begun at 07.30 hours with an irksome motorway drive to the airport with other Monday morning commuters, ending with a few minutes' consternation trying to find a place in the staff car park.

Inside the bowels of the aviation ops centre at Stansted staff paused cheerfully to say, 'Morning, captain', as we passed through. Their bonhomie was genuine. A visit to operations to collect a flight dispatch brief was made. It was all part of the pre-flight ritual for the captain and his first officer.

Flight 910 is no different. Included in the meteorological briefing is the weather along the route, both actual and forecast, the upper winds, temperatures, fixed-time forecast chart for the tropopause level and positions of any weather systems that may affect the route to Nice. With the Significant Weather Conditions (SIGMET), the captain also collects the Computerised Pilot's Log (PLOG). This gives the estimated load sheet, fuel on board (FOB), take-off and landing weight of the aircraft, the slot for departure and the route, including turning-points, forecast winds, ground speeds and *en route* diversions (divs).

Our outbound route is via Detling, Lydd, TOC, BENBO (a mid-point in the Channel) and on over France a few miles west of Dieppe. Some of the acronyms – RBT, PTV, NEV, THR, AGREV, MTL, TOD, AMFOU, PIXOT, DRAMO and LFMN – sound more like a computer language. There are also details on fuel consumption and reserves for diversion and fuel load calculations, flight times and distances. Everything is dutifully digested and signed for. It all appears cursory and perfunctory, but the captain's years of experience born and nurtured in the airline business means nothing is missed.

Final rendezvous with the first officer and the three stewardesses, who are the cabin crew for the flight to Nice, is made upstairs in a crew room overlooking the ramp. The captain briefs the stewardesses on the route weather: 'There's a weather front along the south coast so it might be a little turbulent as we climb. Then it should be smooth all the way. You won't need any suntan lotion because it is four degrees in Nice and overcast!'

Then out to the aircraft. The first officer is going to fly the first leg, to Nice, with the captain flying the return leg. This is decided quite democratically as we pass through the security check. First officers and captains fly leg and leg about, ensuring that both get equal aircraft-handling practice. Friendly greetings are exchanged with the crew coming off duty at the foot of the steps leading from the aircraft. Fox India has just been flown in from Frankfurt.

'Everything OK?'

'Yes, no problems at all', is the reassuring rejoinder. Once in his seat the captain does his cockpit checks and keys in the flight plan, routes, etc. into the Flight Management System (FMS). The FMS, through the aircraft computers, feeds the instruments, the auto-pilot and the two auto-throttles. There's double redundancy computer kit on the flight deck – the FMS 'knows' every airport intimately, every navigation aid, every way-point and every go-around procedure. If an emergency should arise the computers can instantly reveal the nearest five alternative airports on consoles. Meanwhile, the first officer walks the aircraft, checks the tyres and makes sure all panels are fastened. All this is literally behind us now as we soar through several thousand feet into the clear blue over Essex. In the distance a Boeing 747 gracefully curves away towards its home airport, the sun glinting on its white and blue fuselage. As we level out, our ground speed passes 319 knots. True Air Speed is 362 knots, HDG is 207°. The weather front is further in than anticipated. Now the first officer transfers the flying to the capable hands of the auto-pilot. The captain listens out on Paris Volmet for updated weather *en route* (we now have a 50-knot tailwind), and then with the ETA from the FMS he calculates the fuel reserves, or a new burn, using a hand-held calculator.

Fuel calculations will be done twice more before we land. Although these are continually computed through the FMS, nothing so important is taken for granted. In the airline business fuel is one of the most critical considerations. To land with less than minimum landing fuel will certainly ruin your career as an airline pilot. 'We will arrive five minutes ahead of schedule with 0.6 of a tonne of fuel spare', says the captain, handing the first officer the *en route* weather as far as Geneva. Everything is done by the book. There are lots of books. One is the Approach Chart Book. Procedures, rules and regulations and the approach chart diagram attached to the centre of the control column are all strictly followed – to the last digit.

At 33,000 feet the electronic display shows an outside static air temperature (SAT) of -57°C, with a total air temperature (TAT), which is the actual temperature at the aircraft skin due to the friction of air rushing over it, of -34°C. From our altitude England falls behind and the Channel is crossed so smoothly and so fast it might just as well be a stream. The River Loire and its tributaries come into view, meandering like blue tentacles on their journeys south to the Massif Central. Off to the left the majestic Alps appear like Baked Alaska on the skyline. A brief discussion determines whether the peak capped with brandy sauce towering above the rest is Mont Blanc, at 4,810 metres (15,772 feet) the highest in France. Amid all the computer technology an old school atlas reveals that it is! No other office window has such a beautiful vista as this. Just south of Lyon now, we are at 33,000 feet and forty-five minutes from Nice, 200 miles distant. The captain programmes the FMS for our arrival.

Our cocooned little world is now shared with the passengers as the captain goes on intercom and in the calm and reassuring manner peculiar to most airline pilots tells them our landing-time and the weather in Nice. What the passengers cannot see is the exacting, yet routine, workload the crew performs. The captain contacts the Air Azur handling agent and informs them of our intent, passenger manifest and other details for the departure flight. The crew now has all the weather information for Nice and the nominated diversion airports. Starting his soliloquy, the first officer outlines his instrument approach into Nice. The captain listens to the brief and checks.

Soon Cap de Antibes, with its white-walled, red-roofed villas of the rich and famous, passes to our left. Then we are out over the hazy blue waters of the Mediterranean. After confirming with the captain, the first officer swings Fox India left onto the VOR/DME letdown. The captain begins the countdown onto Runway OS Right at Nice:

'6 miles. 21 80 [2,180 ft].'
'5 miles 18.60. Looks a little high.' The first officer corrects onto glidepath.
'3 greens.'
'Little bit high still.'
'4 miles. 15.40. Visual. Runway off to the right.'
'3 miles. Turn right to intercept runway QDM. Full flap.'
'Checks complete. Clear to land. Right runway.'

A dull, monosyllabic computer voice announces its own countdown: '200; 100, DECIDE – Minimums, 50, 40, 30, 20 ...' Our F100 glides in, finally touching down smoothly on the tyre-streaked runway until the reverse thrust gently slows our forward motion to a jogging pace. At about half way we commence a graceful turn left and head slowly for the terminal. A marshaller with two red bats directs us to our air bridge. Number one stewardess pops her head through the door and announces, 'Doors to manual.'

We are on the ground only forty-six minutes – time enough to refuel and replenish and have the cabin cleaned. Fox India burned 3.5 tonnes of fuel on the way down. The aircraft is refuelled with another 5.4 tonnes. With thirty-eight tonnes all-up weight it will take a tonne of fuel to get to 25,000 feet. At 15.05, bang on schedule, we taxi out, the captain now at the controls. At the runway intersection he waits like a patient motorist at a junction for an incoming Boeing 737 to land, and then moves out to the threshold. Brakes off, the Tays purr and off we go, wheels rumbling along the runway. Speed builds to 140 knots. 'V1, rotate', says the first officer. The captain pulls the aircraft off manually. 'Positive' is the next call from the first officer. Captain comments, 'Gear up.' We are airborne.

At 300 feet he commands: 'Heading select 140°.' The aircraft begins its smooth turn to the right to follow the Standard Instrument Departure. Over the sea we climb resolutely to 6,000 feet in no time at all. Still climbing in the turn, we fly a parallel course past Nice Airport before we make a turn north. Eighteen minutes after take-off we are at 22,000 feet and on course. To our right is the Po Valley – ahead are the Hautes Alpes. Fuel consumption on take-off was five tonnes per hour. In the cruise it is down to 1.9 tonnes per hour. At 32,000 feet we pass over Grenoble. At 35,000 feet the temperature sinks like a stone. TAT is now -38°C, SAT -60°. It's hard to believe it can be so cold outside. Inside the cabin everyone's quite comfortable at the controlled 8,000 ft. Our ground-speed is 450 knots – over seven miles a minute. At 16.08 hours Paris can be seen off to our left. Even at 35,000 feet we can make out Charles de Gaulle Airport, the Arc de Triomphe and, of course, the Eiffel Tower.

It's time to think about the landing at Stansted. The captain briefs for a Cat.3B auto-land. This means we are simulating the ability to land in 150 metres of fog. Cat.3B landing parameters are 150 metres in fog with a decision to land with visual reference at fifteen feet above the runway – this is set as the decision height into the computer. We are positioning under radar control for our approach to Runway 23 at Stansted. Final checks are completed. The captain presses the overhead button and chimes alert the cabin staff. We begin our descent.

We touch at 15.45, ten minutes ahead of schedule. Thrust reverse is selected running along the runway centreline guided by the ILS. At 60 knots the captain disengages from the auto-pilot. It is a fine day, but crews have to demonstrate their proficiency because, well, you never know.

We are on the chocks at 15.52. Total flight time there and back three hours and forty-nine minutes, chock to chock – 670 nautical miles each way. Total fuel burned, 6.6 tons. It was all perfectly routine, just as it should be, without a critique or discussion, just a mere, 'Thanks everybody.' I wish I could say the same for the last leg of the day – the M11. Now that's another matter!

This airport has one main passenger terminal, near a village called Stansted Mountfitchet. There are three passenger satellites in which the departure gates are situated, two connected to the main terminal by an air-bridge and the other by the Stansted Airport Transit System people-mover. A fourth satellite under construction is scheduled to be finished by mid-2010. The terminal facilities include several bureaux de change, luggage services, shops, restaurants and bars, as well as Internet access. Car hire and taxis can also be arranged from within the terminal building.

The main passenger terminal at Stansted. It is probably the best in London.

The terminal building was designed by Foster Associates with input from the structural engineer Peter Rice, and features a 'floating' roof, supported by a space frame of inverted-pyramid roof trusses, creating the impression of a stylised swan in flight. The base of each truss structure is a 'utility pillar', which provides indirect uplighting illumination and is the location for air-conditioning, water, telecommunications and electrical outlets. The layout of the airport is designed to provide an unobstructed flow for passengers to arrive at the short-stay car park, move through the check-in hall, go through security and on to the departure gates all on the same level.

From 1997 to 2007 Stansted saw rapid expansion of passenger numbers on the back of the boom in low-cost air travel, peaking at twenty-four million passengers in the twelve months to October 2007, but since then passenger numbers have been in decline. Passengers in the twelve months to May 2009 totalled twenty-one million.

Stansted today remains mainly a low-cost airport, with a majority of its flights operated by easyJet and Ryanair, although it still offers many charter flights and

Ryanair is by far the greatest user of Stansted and bases much of its fleet of Boeing 373s there.

a long-haul flight to Kuala Lumpur operated by Air Asia X with an Airbus A340-300 aircraft. Stansted is the third largest airport in Britain by passenger numbers, and is also Britain's third largest freight airport. Ryanair operates more flights from Stansted than any other airport, and offers 106 destinations, both domestic and international in Europe and Northern Africa.

The airfield has a long history, being opened in 1943. RAF Stansted Mountfitchet was used by the Royal Air Force and the United States Army Air Force as a bomber airfield and as a major maintenance depot. Although the official name was Stansted Mountfitchet, the base was known as simply Stansted in both written and spoken form. The station was first allocated to the USAAF Eighth Air Force in August 1942 as 'Station 169', a heavy bomber airfield. As well as an operational bomber base, Stansted was also an ATSC maintenance and supply depot concerned with major overhauls and modification of B-26s. After D-Day these activities were transferred to France, but the base was still used as a supply storage area for the support of aircraft on the continent. After the withdrawal of the Americans on 12 August 1945, Stansted was taken over by the

A World War Two scene at Stansted when the USAAF were based there.

A DC-3 seen at Stansted in the early post-war period.

Air Ministry and used by the RAF for storage purposes. Between March 1946 and August 1947 Stansted was also used for housing German prisoners of war. The Ministry of Civil Aviation finally took control of Stansted in 1949, but the US military returned in 1954 to extend the runway for a possible transfer to NATO, but instead, the airport returned to civil use in 1957 and came under British Airports Authority control in 1966.

Throughout the 1950s and 1960s Stansted was used for passenger flights by very few airlines – Freddie Laker's Air Charter being one of them – but the airfield was the base for the Civil Aviation Authority Flying Unit, and commercial pilots under training regularly used the airfield, either to get their licences, or to keep current. During the 1960s, 70s and early 80s the Fire Service Training School (FSTS) was based on the eastern side of the airfield under the auspices of the Ministry of Transport and Civil Aviation, now the Civil Aviation Authority. The school was responsible for the training of all aviation fire crews for UK airfields, as well as for many overseas countries. Beginning in 1966, after Stansted was placed under BAA control, the airport was used by holiday charter operators wishing to escape the higher costs associated with operating from Heathrow and Gatwick. From the outset, however, BAA and the British government planned to develop Stansted into London's third airport, to relieve Heathrow and Gatwick of excess congestion in the future. The airport's first purpose-built terminal building opened in 1969 – modified wartime buildings having previously been used – and was expanded the next year to handle the growing number of passengers. A

60 years ago you would be queuing at Stansted to catch one of these bone-shakers. It was the early post-war airliner version of the famous Lancaster bomber, hence the name Lancastrian.

The Trident was a popular British airliner in the 1970s. Its third engine made it a very quick, and for the passengers, very quite.

In 1996 a Sudanese A310 Airbus carrying 197 passengers and crew was hijacked and landed at Stansted. The airport is specially designated and prepared for such eventualities. Skilful negotiations resulted in the safety of all concerned.

major operator from Stansted in the 1960s and early 1970s until it collapsed was Channel Airways Ltd, which also maintained a base at Southend.

Stansted has been the scene of international hijacking dramas three times in recent times. The incidents, which all ended in the surrender of the hijackers, with no injury or loss of life, have established the Essex airport's record for coping with hijacks. Stansted has been specially designated by British authorities to deal with hijacking situations because airliners can be kept well away from terminal buildings and other aircraft while negotiations are carried out. Regular drills also ensure that airport staff and security officers are prepared for dealing with hijacks. In 1982 an Air Tanzania Boeing 737 carrying ninety-nine passengers was seized on an internal flight. It was taken to Nairobi, then Jeddah in Saudi Arabia, followed by Athens, before landing in Stansted. After twenty-six hours of negotiations the passengers were released and the hijackers surrendered. In 1975 a British Airways plane was hijacked *en route* from Manchester to Heathrow. The passengers were let out at Heathrow on the understanding that the hijacker would be flown on to Paris. Instead, the plane actually landed at Stansted, where the hijacker, who had used a toy pistol and imitation dynamite to seize the jet, was arrested. In 1986 Stansted was at the centre of an attempt to kidnap the deposed Nigerian Transport Minister Umaru Dikko and smuggle him out of Britain. The millionaire was found unconscious in a crate at the airport, having been drugged and bound for transport to a show trial in Nigeria. In August 1996 six Iraqi nationals took control of a Sudanese A130 Airbus and forced it to land at the airport. The aircraft, carrying 197 passengers and crew, was hijacked during a flight between Khartoum and Amman. The Airbus was diverted to Stansted, where armed police, supported by potential SAS back-up, were called in, but teams of skilled negotiators prevented the need to storm the aircraft, and the passengers and crew were finally released. The Iraqis, armed with sauce bottles disguised as grenades, knives and claiming to have TNT explosive, said they were seeking refuge from Saddam Hussein's regime. They were jailed at the Old Bailey for between five and nine years, but were later cleared and freed by the Court of Appeal in December 1998.

In 1984 the government approved a plan to develop Stansted in two phases, involving both airfield and terminal improvements that would increase the airport's capacity to fifteen million passengers per year. Construction of the current terminal building began in 1988 and was completed in March 1991, designed by the internationally acclaimed Lord Foster. At the time it was the most modern airport complex in the world, and cost £100 million.

Long-haul scheduled services commenced in the early 1990s when American Airlines operated a transatlantic service between Stansted and Chicago. However, the route was unprofitable and was withdrawn in 1993. Continental Airlines also operated services in the late 1990s from Newark, but this service was stopped shortly after the 11 September 2001 attacks. Long-haul services to the USA returned in late 2005 when Eos Airlines and MAXjet Airways commenced all-business-class

There are many aircraft repair and servicing facilities around Stansted's perimeter.

The view from the control tower.

The people carrier to the furthest gates on the apron side of the terminal.

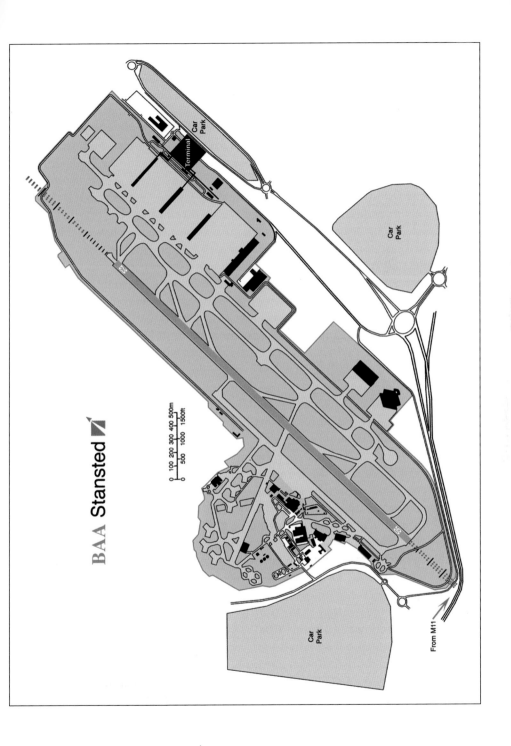

BAA Stansted

Terminal Car Park

Car Park

Car Park

From M11

0 100 200 300 400 500m
0   500   1000   1500ft

services from Stansted to New York-JFK Airport. In 2006 MAXjet expanded its service with flights to Washington DC, Las Vegas and Los Angeles. American Airlines began daily flights to Stansted in October 2007 from New York-JFK, and was originally expected to operate a second daily flight from April 2008. However, all three services to the USA have since been discontinued following the demise of MAXjet Airways in December 2007 and Eos Airlines in April 2008. Finally, in July 2008 American Airlines withdrew from the airport, signalling the end of Stansted transatlantic passenger operations. Stansted also had scheduled and charter flights to Toronto, Montreal and Vancouver, but these flights to Canada have now ceased. Long-haul services to Asia commenced in March 2009 with the Malaysian low-cost airline Air Asia X providing direct flights to Kuala Lumpur.

Stansted, like many other airports around the country, has to deal with noise complaints, often from people who may have only recently moved into the area. The airport management actively tries to sensibly and tactfully deal with complaints. Since 1984 the airport's capacity had been limited to a maximum throughput of twenty-five million passengers per annum in accordance with recommendations made by the 1984 public inquiry and confirmed by the government of the day. A major expansion programme to the existing terminal took place between 2007 and 2009, adding nearly 5,900 square metres of floor area to give space for additional baggage carousels, a new immigration and passport control hall and an arrivals hall with improved facilities.

In November 2006 Uttlesford District Council rejected a BAA planning application to increase the permitted number of aircraft movements and to remove the limit on passenger numbers. BAA immediately appealed against the decision, and a public inquiry was launched that lasted from May to October 2007. The Planning Inspector made his recommendations in January 2008, and these were largely followed by Geoff Hoon, the Secretary of State for Transport, and Hazel Blears, the Secretary of State for Communities and Local Government, who jointly allowed the applicant's Appeal in October 2008. A series of legal challenges by the community campaign group 'Stop Stansted Expansion', formed in 2002 as a working group of the North-West Essex and East Herts Preservation Association, were rejected by the High Court during 2009. SSE has 7,000 members, including more than a hundred local authorities and other organisations. It actively campaigns against what its members see as the unsustainable expansion of the airport. On 24 May 2010, with a change of government in the UK, BAA withdrew its application to build a second runway at Stansted.

Summary of Airports and Other Locations

Although every effort has been made by the authors to ensure that all the facts contained in this book are accurate at the time of going to press, details do change, so the reader is strongly advised to double-check before travelling. The authors and publisher cannot be held responsible for any data that may change over time.

Gatwick

Description: Many airlines use Gatwick for flights to and from the USA because of restrictions on transatlantic operations from Heathrow. The airport is a secondary hub for British Airways and Virgin Atlantic.

Location: Between Horley in Surrey and Crawley in West Sussex, about midway between London and Brighton.

Directions: The airport is accessed by a motorway spur road at Junction 9A of the M23, which links to the main M23 motorway one mile east at Junction 9. The M23 connects with London's orbital motorway. The M25, nine miles north, gives access to Greater London and the South-East. The M23 is the main route by traffic to reach the airport. Gatwick is accessed locally by the A23, which serves Horley and Redhill to the north and Crawley and Brighton to the south. The A217 provides access northwards to the local town of Reigate.

Comments: Two terminals, designated as north and south, are equipped with business lounges, shops and restaurants, landside and airside. Disabled passengers can travel through all areas. There are facilities for baby changing and feeding, and play areas and video games for children. Business travellers have lounges offering business facilities. The South Terminal is spread over 120,000 square metres, of which 14,768 square metres are dedicated to retail facilities. The North Terminal is spread over 75,000 square metres, of which retail facilities constitute 12,530 square metres. The North Terminal consists of an international departure lounge spread over two floors. It also includes arrivals and check-in areas. The avenue consists of shops, food and drink outlets and other amenities. The arrivals area consists of a baggage reclaim area, airline desks, cash machines and shops. Both the South Terminal and the North Terminal are equipped with business lounges, meeting rooms, shops, left baggage and lost property facilities, a currency exchange and duty-free shops. The two terminals have short-term car-parking facilities. Long-term parking is also available. On 31 May 2008 Virgin Holidays opened V Room, Gatwick's first dedicated lounge for leisure travellers. Use of this lounge is exclusive to Virgin Holidays customers flying from the airport to Orlando, Las Vegas and the Caribbean with sister airline Virgin Atlantic. There is also a conference and business centre. Furthermore, the airport and area has hotels from executive to a capsule hotel.

The airport has long- and short-stay car parks – at the airport and off site – although these are often full in summer. Local planning restrictions limit car parking at and around Gatwick.

Gatwick Airport Railway Station is next to the South Terminal and provides connections along the Brighton Main Line to London Victoria and London Bridge Stations, as well as Brighton and Worthing to the south. Gatwick Express to Victoria is the best-known service from the station, but other companies, including Southern, First Capital Connect and First Great Western also use the station. First Capital Connect provides direct trains to Luton Airport, and First Great Western trains provide a direct rail link with Reading and connections with Oxford and the West. Foot passengers can reach Heathrow by an X26 Express Bus from outside East Croydon Station. National Express Coaches operates coaches to Heathrow Airport and Stansted Airport, as well as cities and towns throughout the region and country. Oxford Bus Company operates direct services to Oxford. EasyBus operates mini-coaches from Gatwick to London Victoria. (National Express Dot2Dot used to operate a service to central London, but this ceased in 2008.) Local buses connect the North and South Terminals with Crawley, Horley, Redhill, Horsham and other destinations. Services are offered by Metrobus and

Fastway, a guided-bus rapid transit system, which was the first of its kind to be constructed outside a major city. There are at least two sets of stairs for foot-passengers to leave the South Terminal to ground level (near the cycle route) from Zone L and the railway-station area (steps are labelled Exit Q and Exit P on the ground). These allow access to bus stops for local services.

The North and South Terminals are connected by a three-quarter-mile, elevated, two-way, automated people-mover track. The transit system is normally operated by two automatic, three-car driverless train vehicles. Although colloquially referred to widely as a 'monorail', the transit system runs on a dual concrete track with rubber tyres and is not technically a monorail. The transit system opened in 1983 when the circular satellite pier was built, connecting the pier to the main terminal building; it was the UK's first automated people-mover system. A second transit track was constructed in 1987 to link to the new North Terminal. The original satellite transit line was later replaced with a walkway and travelator link, but the north–south transit remains in operation today. Adtranz C-100 people-mover cars remained in continuous operation until 2009, in which time they travelled a total of two and a half million miles. In September 2009 the vehicles were withdrawn from service to allow the transit system to be upgraded. Meanwhile, the two terminals are connected by a temporary free bus service. A new operating system and transit cars consisting of six Bombardier CX-100 vehicles are being installed, and the guideway and transit stations are being refurbished at a cost of £45 million. They are due for completion in August 2010.

The main runway operates with a Category III Instrument Landing System. The northern runway does not have an instrument landing system, and when it is in use, arriving aircraft use a combination of distance-measuring equipment and assistance from the approach controller using surveillance radar, or where equipped and subject to operator approval, an RNAV (GNSS) Approach, which is also available for the main runway. On all runways, considerable use is made of continuous-descent approach to minimise environmental effects of incoming aircraft, particularly at night.

Brook House, an immigration removal centre of the UK Border Agency, was opened on 18 March 2009 by the then Home Secretary, Jacqui Smith.

The extension of the airport's North Terminal and the construction of a multi-storey car park are planned. Extra baggage reclaim halls and new check-in facilities will also be provided for the North Terminal, along with parking places for 900 more cars. Other projects in the £1 billion investment programme include renovation of the South Terminal, which includes construction of a new forecourt, allowing the airport to handle new aircraft types. In September 2009 the old transit system connecting the terminals at Gatwick was withdrawn from service and gradually replaced by two new shuttles, costing £45 million. These were fully operational in 2010.

Heathrow

Description: The London Airport.

Location: Fifteen miles west of central London and easily accessible from the M4 and M25 motorways.

Directions: Terminals 1 and 3 are close together at the centre of the airport site. Exit the M4 at Junction 4 or the M25 at Junction 15 and follow signs for Heathrow Terminals 1 and 3. If you are using a satellite navigation system, useful postcodes are TW6 1AP for Terminal 1, and TW6 1QG for Terminal 3. Terminal 4 is in the southern part of the airport site and has a separate entrance. Exit the M25 at Junction 14 and follow signs for Heathrow Terminal 4. If you are coming from the M4, leave at Junction 4b and follow the M25 south to Junction 14. If you are using a satellite navigation system, use the postcode TW6 3XA. Terminal 5 is on the Western Perimeter Road and has its own separate access road, reached from Junction 14 of the M25. If you are coming from the M4, exit at Junction 4b and follow the M25 south to Junction 14. If you are using a satellite navigation system, use the postcode TW6 2GA.

Setting down passengers: There are set-down lanes outside the terminals. You may unload on the terminal forecourt, but waiting is not permitted. Police and airport staff patrol the forecourts and will ask waiting vehicles to move on.

Picking up passengers: If you are meeting someone from a flight you must use the Short-Stay Car Park. Waiting is not permitted on the terminal forecourt.

Unattended vehicles: For security reasons, vehicles should not be left unattended at any time. Any vehicle left unattended outside the terminal will be swiftly removed by the police. A charge is made for recovery, and a parking ticket will also be issued. If the vehicle is not collected on the day it is removed, there will be a further charge for each day's storage.

Parking: The Short-Stay Car Parks for each terminal are signposted from roads into Heathrow and are a short walk from check-in. Heathrow Valet Parking operates from designated drop-off points on the terminal forecourts. Heathrow Long-Stay and Business Parking are located a short courtesy-coach-ride from the terminals.

Petrol stations: Texaco station on the Bath Road (A4) – opposite the main entrance. BP station at Hatton Cross, Great West Road (A30). Esso station on the Southern Perimeter Road.

Trains: To get to central London from Heathrow there are three rail options:

Heathrow Express trains run non-stop every fifteen minutes from Terminals 1 or 3, or twenty-one minutes from Terminal 5 between London Paddington and Heathrow. Tickets can be bought on the Internet, at the station or on board the train. Ticket machines installed at Heathrow and Paddington provide multi-lingual, credit card and through-ticket purchasing facilities. The modern trains have air conditioning, plenty of baggage space, wireless Internet and free TV. You can even use your mobile phone when the train is in a tunnel. Need to relax or work in peace? Every train has a Quiet Zone carriage.

For fares, timetables and special offers, or to book tickets in advance, visit the Heathrow Express website or call 0845 600 15 15 (if calling from the UK) or +44 845 600 15 15 (if calling from abroad). Heathrow Express trains stop at Heathrow Central (for Terminals 1 and 3) and Heathrow Terminal 5. Passengers using Terminal 4 can transfer free to or from Heathrow Central using the Heathrow Connect shuttle.

Trains run between 05.10 and 23.25 from Paddington and between 05.07 and 23.42 from Heathrow. Paddington Station is close to Hyde Park and Oxford Street. From Paddington you can catch trains to the South and West of England or take the London Underground's District, Circle, Bakerloo and Hammersmith and City Lines. You can also connect with the District and

Central Lines at Ealing Broadway. Train times and fares are subject to change – please confirm using the London Underground website, or call +44 (0)20 7222 1234 before travelling.

Heathrow Connect runs half-hourly stopping services between Paddington and Heathrow. Modern, air-conditioned trains run every thirty minutes. The journey between Heathrow Central Railway Station and Paddington takes about twenty-five minutes (travel to Terminal 4 or 5 takes a few minutes more). For timetable information, visit the Heathrow Connect website or call National Rail Enquiries on 0845 748 4950. Trains call at Heathrow Central (for Terminals 1 and 3) and Heathrow Terminal 4. Passengers travelling via Terminal 5 can use Heathrow Express trains for a free transfer to or from Heathrow Central. Please ensure that you buy your ticket at the station before boarding the train. A penalty fare zone operates between Hayes and Harlington and London Paddington.

London Underground (Piccadilly Line) provides the most cost-effective rail route between Heathrow Airport and central London. The journey takes less than an hour and you should not have to wait longer than ten minutes for a train, even off-peak. Heathrow has three London Underground stations – one for Terminals 1 and 3, one each at Terminal 4 and Terminal 5. Terminals 1 and 3 Station is in the central area between the terminals and a few minutes' walk from them via underground walkways. Terminal 4 and Terminal 5 Stations are in the basements of the terminal buildings. All stations are in Travelcard Zone 6. Purchase a Travelcard and you are covered for London buses and some mainline trains too. Tickets are available at all London Underground stations, from ticket offices or machines. Pre-paid Oyster cards can also be used on the London Underground.

Where to catch trains:

Terminals 1 and 3: Heathrow Express and Heathrow Connect trains use Heathrow Central Station. Underground services use Heathrow Terminals 1 and 3 Station. Both are in the central area between the terminals, a few minutes' walk from check-in and arrivals.

Terminal 4: The Heathrow Connect and London Underground Stations are both conveniently located in the basement of the terminal. Heathrow

Express passengers should use Heathrow Connect for a free transfer to Heathrow Central.

Terminal 5: The railway station, conveniently located in the basement of the terminal, is served by Heathrow Express and London Underground trains.

Buses and Coaches: National Express and other operators run services from Heathrow to more than 500 destinations. An extensive bus network operates around Heathrow and to destinations in west London and the Thames Valley. Luxury coaches and buses connect Heathrow with the national rail network at Feltham, Watford, Woking and Reading. Direct bus services operate between Heathrow terminals and a large number of hotels near the airport.

Where to catch coaches:

Terminals 1 and 3: All coach services call at the central bus station, which is a short walk from the terminals and has lifts, escalators and moving walkways to help with the journey. The bus station is open twenty-four hours a day and the travel centre is open from 06.00 to 22.30.

Terminal 4: Coaches arrive and depart from Stops 13 and 14 outside the terminal, at arrivals level. Free transfers to the central bus station and Terminal 5 can be made from Stop 7.

Terminal 5: Coaches arrive and depart from Stops 13–16, outside the terminal at arrivals level. There is a National Express ticket office inside the terminal, at international arrivals. Reading RailAir, Oxford Express and Woking Railair services operate from Stops 10–12. Free transfers to the central bus station and Terminal 4 can be made from Stops 8 and 9.

Taxi services: These operate twenty-four hours a day, 365 days a year, subject to local availability. All taxis take cash, and some accept credit and debit cards. London licensed taxis stop at the taxi ranks outside each Heathrow terminal. In central London, taxis can be hailed on the street or booked through your hotel. The journey to central London takes thirty minutes to one hour. Journeys that are both inside London and within twenty miles of the airport are priced using the taxi meter. The fare for travel outside London should be agreed beforehand with the driver. For more information, visit the Transport for London taxi fares page.

It is illegal for anybody – including a licensed taxi or private hire driver, or operator – to approach you offering a journey for payment. This is known as touting. Always use a licensed private-hire operator or taxi. Licensed private-hire drivers must have a PCO licence or temporary permit. All licensed private-hire vehicles must display the yellow PCO licence disc on the front and rear windscreens. Taxi drivers must wear their distinctive metal driver's badge. All black taxis operating from the official Heathrow taxi rank are licensed.

All licensed taxis are wheelchair accessible. Many include other features to make access easier and to assist those with hearing or sight impediments. Wheelchairs should be secured at all times. Taxis carry assistance dogs at no extra charge.

Comments: All that a traveller could possibly need can be found at the official BAA website at http://www.heathrowairport.com

London City

Description: Ideal for city high-flyers to take off for the weekend.

Directions: London City Airport is linked to London's new financial district at Canary Wharf and to the traditional financial district of the City of London via the Docklands Light Railway and with an interchange to the London Underground. London City Airport DLR Station is situated immediately adjacent to the terminal building, with enclosed access to and from the elevated platforms.

The airport is served by London Bus Services 473 and 474 running to local east London destinations. The airport has both a short-term and a long-term car park, both within walking distance of the terminal, and a taxi rank outside the terminal door. There are plans to rebuild and refurbish the terminal. The exterior of the terminal building will remain the same, but the internal infrastructure will be rebuilt to better utilise the space and handle the projected increase in passenger numbers.

Comments: Inside the terminal there are twenty-two check-in desks, plus self-service kiosks for Air France, British Airways, Lufthansa, VLM Airlines, KLM,

Luxair, Swiss International Air Lines and SAS. There are fourteen gates, with a further four stands to the west connected via an airside bus. The departure lounge – making use of soft, warm materials, including timber and polished limestone floors, marble surfaces and leather seating throughout – is configured with numerous laptop plug-in points and complimentary Wi-Fi access. The lounge offers passengers an uncluttered environment where they can continue to work using smartphone devices or laptops, or relax in tranquillity with the 'silent departure-lounge policy' of no broadcast announcements or boarding calls.

London Luton

Description: A twenty-four-hour, seven-day service with excellent transportation links to both London and the Midlands ensure that London Luton remains the preferred choice for the majority of UK-bound business aviation traffic.

Directions: Road access: To and from the East and A1 via the A505 dual carriageway through Hitchin. The airport lies just off the A505 and is clearly signposted. To and from the M25: If approaching via Dunstable, follow the airport signs. Alternative approaches include travelling via the M40/M25 to join the M1 and then exit via Junction 10. Exit the M25 at Junction 21 for the access to the M1. To and from the M1, just thirty minutes from north London, fifteen minutes from the M25 and five minutes from the M1. The airport is just two miles from the M1 motorway. Exit the M1 at Junction 10. The route to the airport is clearly signposted.

Car Parking: In addition to London Luton's Long-Term Car Park, the airport offers the following parking, drop-off and pick-up options:

Mid-Term Car Park – free drop-off, free pick-up and free parking for up to sixty minutes. Two-minute free bus ride to the terminal.

Short-Term Car Park – drop-off, pick-up and parking. Free disabled parking for up to sixty minutes, four-minute walk to the terminal.
Priority Set-down – drop-off only. Cars must not be left unattended. Two-minute walk to the terminal.

Rail access: The London Luton Parkway Station, making the journey to central London less than thirty minutes. Regular rail services to central London take as little as twenty-one minutes with East Midlands Trains and twenty-five minutes with First Capital Connect. Other destinations include the south coast, the Midlands and northern England.

A shuttle bus service operates to and from Luton Airport Parkway Station; this is normally just a five-minute trip from the airport terminal building. The service runs every ten minutes between 05.00 and midnight, and also connects with all trains calling at Luton Airport Parkway overnight. Please check train times for details. Rail passengers will be able to purchase through-tickets to London Luton Airport. Those passengers arriving at Luton Airport Parkway Station without a through-ticket to the airport and wish to use the shuttle bus will pay an excess charge each way if they arrive at the station by train. Passengers arriving at the airport or at the station without purchasing a rail ticket will pay a bus fare (children half price).

Bus and Coach access: Luton Airport has excellent connections with key towns and cities across the country. The coach pick-up and drop-off points and bus bays are situated in front of the terminal building. Green Line 757 provides an express coach link between London Luton Airport and central London from Bays 10 and 11. National Express services depart from Bays 4, 5 and 6 to destinations across the UK. easyBus offers a high-frequency, low-cost express bus service between central London and Luton Airport. easyBus coaches run twenty-four hours a day between the airport and central London. There are stops at Brent Cross, Finchley Road, Baker Street, Oxford Street/Marble Arch and London Victoria. Virgin Rail Link operates from Bay 7 and runs an express service to Milton Keynes Station. This dedicated airport coach link service runs from Milton Keynes Railway Station direct to the airport terminal. Conveniently timed to connect with Virgin Trains services to/from the West Midlands and the West, the service runs hourly from early until late, seven days each week.

Comments: Luton Airport has launched 'Flying for Success' (F4S), a project in partnership with Luton Borough Council. F4S involves inviting groups of local primary school children to make educational visits that allow the children to gain and develop essential numeracy and literature skills in an environment that is stimulating and exciting, and therefore conducive to learning. Someries and Wigmore Junior schools were first to be invited to the airport, and enjoyed four weeks of unique educational tours, which were themed on Airport Security, Airport Terminal, Airport Fire Service and Airport Ecology.

Terminal facilities: W.H. Smith offers everything you need for your journey, from a travel adaptor to a toothbrush. Gamegrid offers entertainment and games, International Currency Exchange (ICE) offers currency exchange, BT and International phone cards and travel insurance. The Marks and Spencer Simply Food concept offers fresh and convenient food in convenient locations and a range of food and wine for later. Rolling Luggage offers top brands of travel luggage and luggage accessories, including Samsonite and Travelpro. There is the Spectrum Internet Café situated in the Check-In Concourse. Equipped with large 17 in. screens where you can surf the Web, check e-mails and play online games, payable by sterling or euro coins and most major credit cards. The Change Group offers currency exchange, BT and International phone cards and travel insurance. Tie Rack is a specialist designer retailer with focus on high-quality ties, scarves and fashion accessories.

Website: http://www.london-luton.co.uk

Flight Information: http://www.london-luton.co.uk/en/flights.asp

Stansted

Description: Britain's third largest airport. The main terminal building is located on the south-east side of the airport and has a very different layout from many other airports, especially within the UK. The terminal is an oblong glass building, which is separated into three areas – Check-in Concourse, Arrivals and Departures. There are no gates in the main terminal; instead, there are three separate oblong satellite buildings in which the gates are located. Two satellite buildings are reached by the Stansted Airport Transit System, which takes passengers to and from the departure hall in the terminal building. The third satellite building is not operated by the transit system, but is connected to the terminal building by a walkway. The future fourth satellite building is likely to be reached by the transit trains; it will be too far for passengers to walk. The transit system connects two of the terminals via a two-mile free automated people-mover service that runs on a dual concrete track. The system uses a mix of Adtranz C-100 and Bombardier CX-100 vehicles to carry passengers to departure gates; unlike the similar Gatwick Airport transit, the Stansted transit is only accessible 'airside' (i.e. only after passengers pass through security). A corporate jet centre on the north-west side of the airport is used for private and executive flying.

Directions: London Stansted is connected to north-east London and Cambridge by the M11 motorway and to Braintree, Colchester and Harwich by the A120 dual carriageway. This airport has its own dedicated railway station located below the main terminal building, with frequent rail services to Cambridge, Leicester and the Midlands, operated by CrossCountry. The Stansted Express train runs to and from Liverpool Street Station in London every fifteen minutes, and the journey time is forty-five minutes to one hour. A Monday–Saturday hourly service operates to Harlow and Stratford, London, calling at most stations.

The airport is well served by a network of local and longer-distance bus and coach routes. There are scheduled express services that run to and from Stratford, Victoria Coach Station, Liverpool Street Station and Golders Green, costing about half the train fare but taking longer. The bus station is next to the terminal building. National Express runs scheduled but infrequent direct coach services to the airport from Oxford as Service JL737, taking about three hours, and hourly services to and from Cambridge. easyBus and Terravision provide journeys between the airport and central London. Excel operates a coach service to Capel St Mary and Ipswich every two hours, twenty-four hours a day. This service operates as Airdirect. Also, a new route has been introduced linking Stansted Airport to Grays via Brentwood, Ongar and Basildon, called Route X3, operating twenty-four hours a day, every two hours. FirstGroup operates a service between the airport and Clacton-on-Sea, the X22 service departing every two hours, seven days a week, excluding Christmas Day. A few local bus services operate to the nearby communities of Bishops Stortford, Stansted Mountfitchet and connect to many of the nearby villages.

Comments: Short-term car parking and passenger drop-off is located directly outside the passenger terminal. There are long-term car parks situated a distance from the terminal, so passengers need to allow at least twenty minutes to park and use a courtesy-bus shuttle service prior to check-in.

The Servisair Executive Lounge is available to all passengers flying from Stansted Airport for a small charge; it is not exclusively for business or corporate travellers. The Executive Lounge in the airport offers complimentary alcoholic and soft drinks plus snacks. Magazines and newspapers are also available, along with credit card payphones. This lounge implements a smart/casual dress code by all passengers. Children under the age of 12 are not permitted in the lounge. Flight announcements are not available in the Suite, just unofficial flight information on screens, so do check the time of your flight and have ample time to get to your boarding-gate.

Passengers will find wireless Internet access points throughout the airport. Providers of this service are T-Mobile, BT Openzone and The Cloud Networks. Wireless-compatible laptops or handheld computers can be used to connect instantly to the Internet within these wireless hotspots. Most modern computers have a built-in wireless LAN (Local Area Network) card, and many can be upgraded using a wireless networking card. The service works through your usual Web browser, optimised for Internet Explorer 5 or Internet Pocket Explorer. Your device should run recent Microsoft Windows software. How to connect? Follow these simple steps: When in the passenger terminal, turn on your wireless-enabled device. Most laptops include Intel Centrino wireless functionality as standard. Other laptops may need a separate card, which you can purchase from any major electronics shop. Launch your browser and select the preferred wireless network from the icons on the screen when the service is automatically detected. The Cloud Networks can connect you through a growing range of service providers, e.g. O2, Skype for Internet telephone calls and Nintendo for online DS gaming.

Enter your normal username and password when prompted to finalise connection. If you do not own an account with one of the airport service providers, it is possible to sign up securely online, or in advance from their websites. T-Mobile laptop stations for flat batteries are located throughout the airport; these provide instant power via a dedicated workstation environment. Step-by-step log-on instructions are provided.

Travel between airports

London Gatwick

By coach: National Express operates the only direct link between Heathrow and Gatwick Airports, with up to six services per hour. Tickets can be purchased online, from National Express ticket desks or from the coach driver. The journey time is approximately seventy-five minutes. To book tickets and for timetable information, call +44 (0)871 781 8181 or visit the National Express website.

By train: Gatwick Express operates between London Victoria and Gatwick Airport. Victoria can be reached from central London by taxi, bus or Underground (District, Circle and Victoria Lines). Non-stop Gatwick Express trains run every fifteen minutes, and the journey takes thirty minutes to Gatwick South Terminal. A free transit service to the North Terminal stops upstairs from the rail platforms. You can travel by rail to Gatwick from Feltham by changing at Clapham Junction. The 285 bus operates between Heathrow central bus station and Feltham.

For more information visit the Gatwick Express website.

Stansted

By coach: National Express coaches offer the only direct link between Heathrow and Stansted airports, with departures every thirty to sixty minutes. The journey time is approximately ninety minutes. For further information, call +44 (0)871 781 8181 or visit the National Express website.

By train: Stansted Express operates trains between London Liverpool Street and Stansted Airport. Liverpool Street can be reached from central London by taxi, bus or Underground (Circle, Metropolitan and Hammersmith and City Lines). Alternatively, avoid central London by connecting with the Stansted Express at Tottenham Hale, which is on the London Underground Victoria Line. Stansted Express trains run every fifteen or thirty minutes, and the journey takes about forty-six minutes. For more information visit the Stansted Express website.